TAMIL FOR BEGINNERS

notionpress
.com

TAMIL FOR BEGINNERS

READ & WRITE!

MALARVIZHI

notionpress.com

Notion Press

Old No. 38, New No. 6
McNichols Road, Chetpet
Chennai - 600 031

First Published by Notion Press 2018

ISBN 978-1-64429-978-4

Dedicated to

My Guru,

the human form of the Supreme Being in my heart,

who fills my eyes with tears

and my life with joy

at the mere thought of

His infinite compassion.

தமிழ் பயில்வோம்

அறிவோம் செந்தமிழ்
ஆறுமுகன் அருளோடு! நாம்
இணைவோம் தமிழால், மொழி
ஈன்ற அன்னை போலாம்!
உயர்வோம் நாம் தமிழ்க் கற்று!
ஊடுருவும் நம்முள் மொழிப்பற்று!
எங்கும் தமிழ் உணர்வோடு
ஏகுவோம் மேலும் சிறப்புற்று!
ஐம்பொறியிலும் தமிழை
ஒரு முகமாய் அகத்தில் பற்றுவோம்!
ஓய்ந்திடாது சிந்தித்தால்
ஔடதமாகும் அமுதத் தமிழாம்!
அஃதே அருந்தமிழின் புகழாம்!

Let's Learn Tamil

Let's learn classical Tamil
With the grace of the Six-faced God
Let's come together in unison with Tamil being our reason
Let's value this language like our own Mother
Through learning Tamil, let's progress forward
And devotion towards Tamil shall penetrate our spirits.
Along with our Tamil sentiments,
We shall increasingly refine ourselves.
Through our five senses,
Let's converge our focus upon Tamil and grasp its essence.
If unwaveringly contemplated
The nectar of Tamil would become the ultimate remedy
And therein lies the true glory of Tamil!

Preface

Why this thamizhveri?

As a mother...

A decade ago, I was residing in California and I was thinking about coming back with my family to settle down in India. Since I am a Tamilian, I wanted my children to know and cultivate their Tamil roots. For lack of instruction medium, I took up the task of teaching my daughter (my son being only an infant at the time) the basics of reading and writing in a way that could be easily grasped. It was successful in building a strong foundation. My daughter started familiarizing herself with words from the dictionary and could read little stories. On coming back, I realized that Tamil was compulsory in schools upto a certain grade and she had joined at a stage where the standard was past the basics. In regard to this, her initial learning with me was highly useful to pick up on her studies without too much of a hastle.

As a tutor...

In more recent times, I have conducted private Tamil tuitions, over the course of which I became aware of the learning difficulties of non-Tamil speakers from other states of India and abroad. Having no background in Tamil can be tough for those who join a new school in Tamil Nadu after 4th grade or come for a a temporary project for a few years. Furthermore, most supplements that exist in the market do not satisfactorily pass on the elementary basics in an engaging way. This book is intended to be useful for school children who have had the neccessity to opt Tamil as their second/third language as well as English speaking Tamil enthusiasts.

With my experience as a parent and as a tutor, I know the importance of a strong foundation, that is simple and clear, because it reduces the reluctance of people and motivates them to read more. This book is intended as a seed towards Tamil learning in a fun and easily comprehensible manner that reinforces the basics for debutants of any age group and eventually encourage self-learning.

This book focuses only on the basics. We start from scratch by identifying, writing and reading out the letters. Phonetics of certain letters are unique with no equivalents in English, but can be grasped with a little bit of extra effort.

Progression in this manual is based on 3 parts to facilitate your learning. These parts refer to the Tamil consonants which are divided into 3 catogories/types as follows:

1.Vallinam 2. Idaiyinam 3. Mellinam

This particular structure will help you organise your learning more easily instead of memorization of all letters in one go.

The unsurpassable beauty and depth of this more than 2000-year-old ancient and classical language is often masked by the initial difficulties and complexities of learning it, for both Tamil and non-Tamil speaking populations, often discouraging and demotivating people from pursuing it. For most of them, these difficulties stem from an inadequate comprehension of the letters and so, it is in my highest hopes that this book would be an ideal aid if not the solution to a healthy and insightful beginning to all your future progress.

I would like to offer my honest and sincere gratitude to my well-wisher Ram for His guidance. Thanks to my daughter for helping me design this book.

All the best and happy learning!

- Malarvizhi

Contents

Introduction to Tamil Letters	x
Approach to Writing Letters	2
Trace all the Letters	4
Activity on Vowels	5
Consonants Type 1: Vallinam	6
Activity I	18
Consonants Type 2: Idaiyinam	20
Activity II	32
Consonants Type 3: Mellinam	34
Activity III	46
Exercise Using all Tamil Letters	48
Ayudha Letter	52
Special Letters	53
Answer Key	54
Table of Tamil Letters	55
Game	56
Alligator Challenges	59
Rangu's Guide!	60
Guide to Training Hut Activity (C)	65

INTRODUCTION TO TAMIL LETTERS

உயிர் எழுத்துக்கள் - 12 | Vowels - 12

a	ā	i	ī	u	ū	e	ē	ai	o	ō	au
அ	ஆ	இ	ஈ	உ	ஊ	எ	ஏ	ஐ	ஒ	ஓ	ஔ

ஆயுத எழுத்து - ஃ (ahk) - 1 | Āyudha Ezhuthu - 1

மெய் எழுத்துக்கள் - 18 | Consonants - 18

k	ṅ	ch	ñ	ṭ	ṇ	th	n	p
க்	ங்	ச்	ஞ்	ட்	ண்	த்	ந்	ப்
m	y	r	l	v	zh	ḷ	ṛ	ṉ
ம்	ய்	ர்	ல்	வ்	ழ்	ள்	ற்	ன்

சிறப்பு எழுத்துக்கள் - 6 | Special Letters - 6

Ja	sa	sha	ha	ksha	sri	(sound of letters from other languages)
ஜ	ஸ	ஷ	ஹ	க்ஷ	ஸ்ரீ	(பிற மொழி எழுத்துக்கள் சிலவற்றின் ஒலி குறிப்பன)

தமிழ் எழுத்துக்கள் — Tamil Letters

உயிரெழுத்துக்கள்	= 12	(Uyir Ezhuthu) Vowels	= 12
மெய்யெழுத்துக்கள்	= 18	(Mei Ezhuthu) Consonants	= 18
ஆயுத எழுத்து	= 1	Ayudha Ezhuthu	= 1

Consonants (18) are divided into 3 types as follows based on ease of pronunciation (1- hard; 2 - midrange; 3 - soft):

1. வல்லினம் - க ச ட த ப ற — Vallinam - ka cha ta tha pa ṛa
2. இடையினம் - ய ர ல வ ழ ள — Idaiyinam - ya ra la va zha ḷa
3. மெல்லினம் - ங ஞ ண ந ம ன — Mellinam - ṅa ña ṇa na ma ṉa

Pronounce Vowels (12) with the help of English words:

அ / a as in America/Arabia — ஆ / ā as in On / Arch

இ / i as in Ink / India — ஈ / ī as in Eel / East

உ / u as in Full / Uttar Pradesh — ஊ / ū as in Ooze / Ooty

எ / e as in Enter / Elephant — ஏ / ē as in Angel / Asia

ஐ / ai as in Eye/Island

ஒ / o as in Orissa/ Olympic — ஓ / ō as in Ozone / Oats

ஔ / au as in Owl / Auvai Pātti

- Kuril sounds/ Short sounds — - Nedil Sounds/ Long Sounds

How to Write Tamil Vowels

How to Write Tamil Consonants

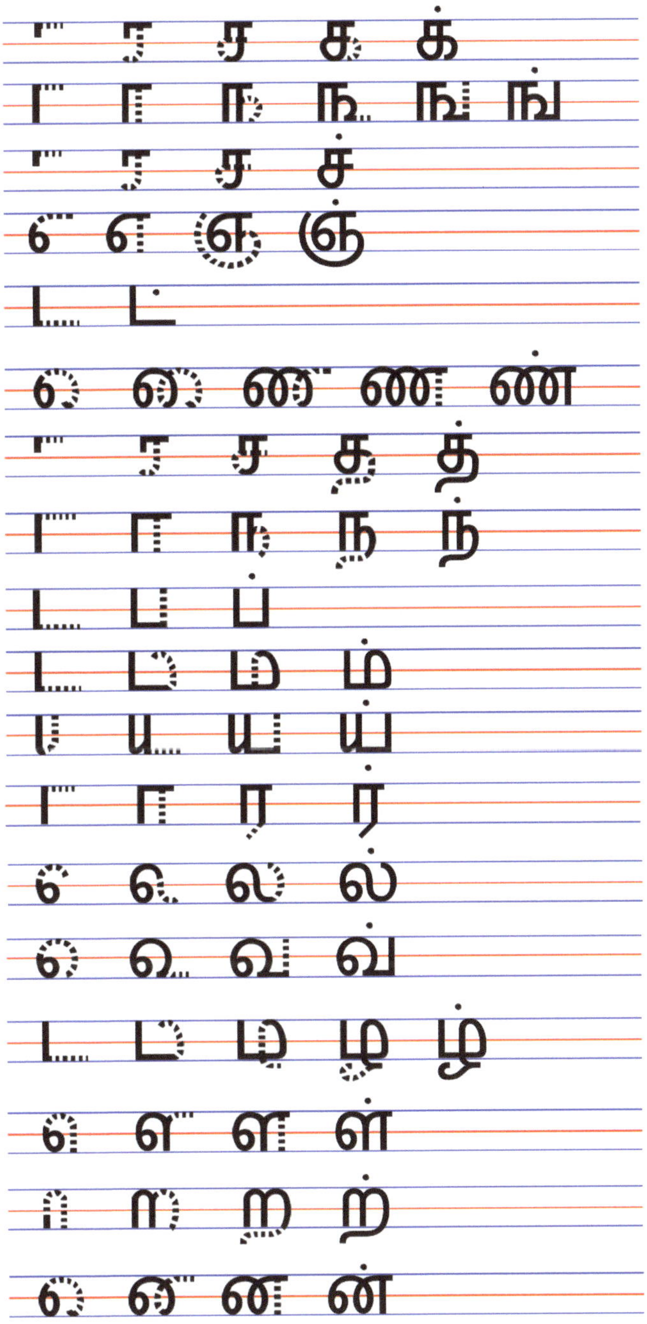

க்	(k/g)
ங்	(ṅ)
ச்	(ch/s)
ஞ்	(ñ)
ட்	(ṭ/ḍ)
ண்	(ṇ)
த்	(th/dh)
ந்	(n)
ப்	(p/b)
ம்	(m)
ய்	(y)
ர்	(r)
ல்	(l)
வ்	(v)
ழ்	(zh)
ள்	(ḷ)
ற்	(ṛ)
ன்	(ṉ)

Trace all the Letters

அ	ஆ	இ	ஈ	உ	ஊ
எ	ஏ	ஐ	ஒ	ஓ	ஔ
க	ங	ச	ஞ	ட	ண
த	ந	ப	ம	ய	ர
ல	வ	ழ	ள	ற	ன
ஜ	ஸ	ஷ	ஹ	க்ஷ	ஸ்ரீ

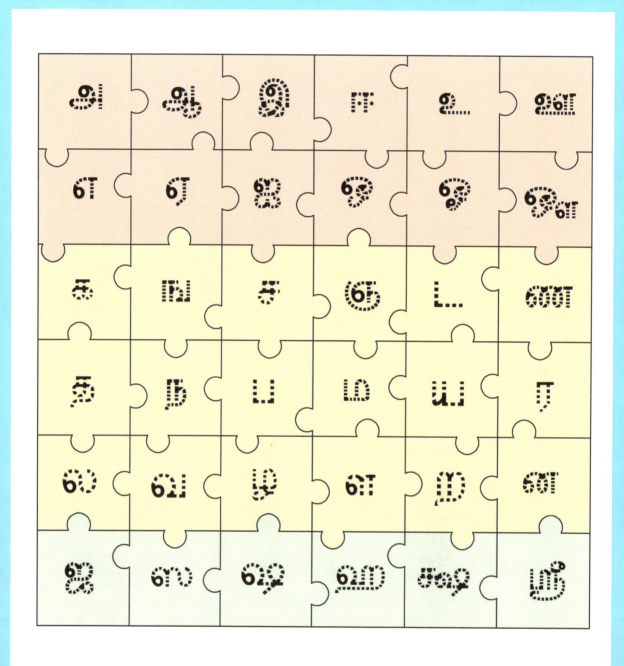

Fill in the short sounding vowels for the baby elephant and long sounding vowels for the big elephant.

அ இ உ எ ஒ

ஆ ஈ ஊ ஏ ஐ ஓ ஔ

LESSON - பாடம்

கற்போம் வல்லினம் /KAṞPŌM VALLIṈAM / Let us learn Vallinam

க் வரிசை -------------- (i)k/(i)g Series

க் + அ = க	(i)k + a = ka	க் + எ = கெ	(i)k + e = ke
க் + ஆ = கா	(i)k + ā = kā	க் + ஏ = கே	(i)k + ē = kē
க் + இ = கி	(i)k + i = ki	க் + ஐ = கை	(i)k + ai = kai
க் + ஈ = கீ	(i)k + ī = kī	க் + ஒ = கொ	(i)k + o = ko
க் + உ = கு	(i)k + u = ku	க் + ஓ = கோ	(i)k + ō = kō
க் + ஊ = கூ	(i)k + ū = kū	க் + ஔ = கௌ	(i)k + au = kau

குறில்/ kuril / short sound   நெடில்/ nedil / long sound

க் / 'k' as in pick / 'g' as in big

க	/	'ka' as in come	/	'ga' as in gum
கா	/	'kā' as in card	/	'gā' as in god
கி	/	'ki' as in kit	/	'gi' as in gift
கீ	/	'kī' as in key	/	'gī' as in ghee
கு	/	'ku' as in cook	/	'gu' as in Gujarat
கூ	/	'kū' as in cool	/	'gū' as in google
கெ	/	'ke' as in kettle	/	'ge' as in get
கே	/	'kē' as in cave	/	'gē' as in gate
கை	/	'kai' as in kind	/	'gai' as in guide
கொ	/	'ko' as in Columbia	/	'go' as in Gorilla
கோ	/	'kō' as in code	/	'gō' as in goal
கௌ	/	'kau' as in cow	/	'gau' as in gown

N.B.
All consonants of the Vallinam group (except 'ற்' group) have dual pronunciations. This does not mean that for one given word, both possibilities would be correct. The word itself and generally the position of the letter in the word determines which option is to be used. There are no hard and fast universal rules that control this and it is only through hearing and speaking Tamil that you can get a hang of using the appropriate pronunciation.

பயிற்சி – EXERCISES

Hierarchy of Skill Acquisition through the following exercises
I. Formation of the letter ♦ II. Correlation of sounds ♦ III. Differentiating between long and short sounds
IV. Reading words as a combination of vowels and consonants of the current series ♦ V. Series Recap

I. Learn to write by tracing the dotted lines completing each character. X = க

X	Xா	Xி	Xீ	*	*
க	கா	கி	கீ	கு	கூ
ெX	ேX	ைX	ொX	ோX	ௌX
கெ	கே	கை	கொ	கோ	கௌ

II. Listen to the sound of the word and write its closest equivalent Tamil letter.

COW - ☐ GUY - ☐

GO - ☐ KEY - ☐

III. Fill in the missing kuril/nedil letters in this incomplete series.

க	☐	☐	கீ	கு	☐
☐	கே	கை	☐	கோ	கௌ

IV. Read aloud the given words.

அக்கா /AKKĀ/sister **கை**/KAI/ hand **ஈகை**/ĪGAI/ charity

கொக்கு/KOKKU/ crane **காக்கை**/KĀKKAI/ crow **எஃகு**/EKGU/ iron metal

கொக்கி/KOKKI/ hook **ஊக்கு**/ŪKKU/ pin **காக்க** /KĀKKA/ protect

V. Fill in the letters of the (i)k series.

க் Series = க் + (அ, ஆ, இ, ஈ, உ, ஊ, எ, ஏ, ஐ, ஒ, ஓ, ஔ)

= ____,____,____,____,____,____,____,____,____,____,____,____

* - The dotted lines on the 'x' are not shown for the 'u' and 'u' characters as the indication is not generic for all letters.

LESSON - பாடம்

கற்போம் வல்லினம் /KAṞPŌM VALLIṈAM / Let us learn Vallinam

ச் வரிசை -------------- (i)ch/(i)s Series

ச் + அ = ச	(i)ch + a = cha	ச் + எ = செ	(i)ch + e = che
ச் + ஆ = சா	(i)ch + $\bar{a}$ = ch$\bar{a}$	ச் + ஏ = சே	(i)ch + $\bar{e}$ = ch$\bar{e}$
ச் + இ = சி	(i)ch + i = chi	ச் + ஐ = சை	(i)ch + ai = chai
ச் + ஈ = சீ	(i)ch + $\bar{i}$ = ch$\bar{i}$	ச் + ஒ = சொ	(i)ch + o = cho
ச் + உ = சு	(i)ch + u = chu	ச் + ஓ = சோ	(i)ch + $\bar{o}$ = ch$\bar{o}$
ச் + ஊ = சூ	(i)ch + $\bar{u}$ = ch$\bar{u}$	ச் + ஔ = சௌ	(i)ch + au = chau

குறில்/ kuril / short sound   நெடில்/ nedil / long sound

ச் / 'ch' as in rich / 's' as in is

ச	/ 'cha'	as in	chunk	/ 'sa'	as in	sun
சா	/ 'ch$\bar{a}$'	as in	chart	/ 's$\bar{a}$'	as in	salt
சி	/ 'chi'	as in	chimney	/ 'si'	as in	sim
சீ	/ 'ch$\bar{i}$'	as in	cheap	/ 's$\bar{i}$'	as in	seal
சு	/ 'chu'	as in	maturity	/ 'su'	as in	sudoku
சூ	/ 'ch$\bar{u}$'	as in	choose	/ 's$\bar{u}$'	as in	soon
செ	/ 'che'	as in	Chennai	/ 'se'	as in	sell
சே	/ 'ch$\bar{e}$'	as in	chase	/ 's$\bar{e}$'	as in	sale
சை	/ 'chai'	as in	child	/ 'sai'	as in	sign
சொ	/ 'cho'			/ 'so'	as in	solidify
சோ	/ 'ch$\bar{o}$'	as in	nachos	/ 's$\bar{o}$'	as in	soap
சௌ	/ 'chau'	as in	choultry	/ 'sau'	as in	sound

க் ச் ட் த் ப் ற்

பயிற்சி – EXERCISES

Hierarchy of Skill Acquisition through the following exercises

I. Formation of the letter ♦ II. Correlation of sounds ♦ III. Differentiating between long and short sounds

IV. Reading words as a combination of vowels and consonants of the current series ♦ V. Series Recap

I. Learn to write by tracing the dotted lines completing each character. X = ச

X	Xா	Xி	Xீ		
ச	சா	சி	சீ	சு	சூ
ெX	ேX	ைX	ெXா	ேXா	ெXள
செ	சே	சை	சொ	சோ	சௌ

II. Listen to the sound of the word and write its closest equivalent Tamil letter.

SEA - ☐ SAW - ☐ SO - ☐

III. Fill in the missing kuril/nedil letters in this incomplete series.

☐ சா ☐ சீ சு ☐

செ ☐ சை சொ ☐ சௌ

IV. Read aloud the given words.

அசை/ASAI/ move

ஆசை/ĀSAI/ desire

ஆசி/ĀSI/ bless

ஆச்சி/ĀCCHI/ grandma

இசை/ISAI/ music

ஓசை/ŌSAI/ noise

ஏசு/ĒSU/ Jesus

சிசு/SISU/ newborn

ஊசி/ ŪSI/ injection

உச்சி/UCCHI/ peak

அச்சு/ACCHU/mould/print

இச்சை/ICCHAI/ desire

V. Fill in the letters of the 'ச்' series.

ச் Series = ச் + (அ, ஆ, இ, ஈ, உ, ஊ, எ, ஏ, ஐ, ஒ, ஓ, ஔ)

= ____,____,____,____,____,____,____,____,____,____,____,____

LESSON - பாடம்

கற்போம் வல்லினம் /KAṞPŌM VALLIṈAM / Let us learn Vallinam

ட் வரிசை --------------- (i)ṭ/(i)ḍ Series

ட் + அ = ட	(i)ṭ + a = ṭa	ட் + எ = டெ	(i)ṭ + e = ṭe
ட் + ஆ = டா	(i)ṭ + ā = ṭā	ட் + ஏ = டே	(i)ṭ + ē = ṭē
ட் + இ = டி	(i)ṭ + i = ṭi	ட் + ஐ = டை	(i)ṭ + ai = ṭai
ட் + ஈ = டீ	(i)ṭ + ī = ṭī	ட் + ஒ = டொ	(i)ṭ + o = ṭo
ட் + உ = டு	(i)ṭ + u = ṭu	ட் + ஓ = டோ	(i)ṭ + ō = ṭō
ட் + ஊ = டூ	(i)ṭ + ū = ṭū	ட் + ஔ = டௌ	(i)ṭ + au = ṭau

குறில்/ kuril / short sound   நெடில்/ nedil / long sound

ட் / 'ṭ' as in it / 'ḍ' as in kid

ட	/ 'ṭa'	as in tuck	/ 'ḍa'	as in	duck
டா	/ 'ṭā'	as in tall	/ 'ḍā'	as in	dark
டி	/ 'ṭi'	as in tick	/ 'ḍi'	as in	dear
டீ	/ 'ṭī'	as in tea	/ 'ḍī'	as in	deep
டு	/ 'ṭu'	as in today	/ 'ḍu'	as in	Tamil Nadu
டூ	/ 'ṭū'	as in tool	/ 'ḍū'	as in	doomed
டெ	/ 'ṭe'	as in tailor	/ 'ḍe'	as in	delivery
டே	/ 'ṭē'	as in table	/ 'ḍē'	as in	day
டை	/ 'ṭai'	as in type	/ 'ḍai'	as in	dye
டொ	/ 'ṭo'	as in tornado	/ 'ḍo'	as in	domain
டோ	/ 'ṭō'	as in toll	/ 'ḍō'	as in	door
டௌ	/ 'ṭau'	as in town	/ 'ḍau'	as in	down

க் ச் ட் த் ப் ற்

பயிற்சி – EXERCISES

Hierarchy of Skill Acquisition through the following exercises
I. Formation of the letter ♦ II. Correlation of sounds ♦ III. Differentiating between long and short sounds
IV. Reading words as a combination of vowels and consonants of the current series ♦ V. Series Recap

I. Learn to write by tracing the dotted lines completing each character. X = ட

X	Xா	Xி	Xீ		
ட	டா	டி	டீ	டு	டூ
ெX	ேX	ைX	ெXா	ேXா	ெXள
டெ	டே	டை	டொ	டோ	டௌ

II. Listen to the sound of the word and write its closest equivalent Tamil letter.

TIE - ☐ TEA - ☐ DAY - ☐

III. Fill in the missing kuril/nedil letters in this incomplete series.

☐	டா	டி	☐	☐	டூ
☐	டே	டை	டொ	☐	டௌ

IV. Read aloud the given words.

ஆடை/ĀḌAI/ dress
இடை/IḌAI/ middle/hip
உடை/UḌAI/ break/garment
ஓடை/ŌḌAI/ canal
அடி/AḌI/ step/beat
இடி/IḌI/ thunder
ஒடி/OḌI/ break
ஓடு/ŌḌU/ run/shell
ஆடு/ĀḌU/ goat/dance
ஓட்டை/ŌṬṬAI/ hole
எட்டு/EṬṬU/ eight/reach
ஒட்டு/OṬṬU/stick(verb)
ஓட்டு/ŌṬṬU/ drive

V. Fill in the letters of the 'ட்' series.

ட் Series = ட் + (அ, ஆ, இ, ஈ, உ, ஊ, எ, ஏ, ஐ, ஒ, ஓ, ஔ)

= ____, ____, ____, ____, ____, ____, ____, ____, ____, ____, ____, ____

க் ச் ட் த் ப் ற்

LESSON - பாடம்

கற்போம் வல்லினம் /KAṞPŌM VALLIṈAM / Let us learn Vallinam

த் வரிசை --------------- (i)th/(i)dh Series

த் + அ = த	(i)th + a = tha	த் + எ = தெ	(i)th + e = the
த் + ஆ = தா	(i)th + ā = thā	த் + ஏ = தே	(i)th + ē = thē
த் + இ = தி	(i)th + i = thi	த் + ஐ = தை	(i)th + ai = thai
த் + ஈ = தீ	(i)th + ī = thī	த் + ஒ = தொ	(i)th + o = tho
த் + உ = து	(i)th + u = thu	த் + ஓ = தோ	(i)th + ō = thō
த் + ஊ = தூ	(i)th + ū = thū	த் + ஔ = தௌ	(i)th + au = thau

குறில் / kuril / short sound   நெடில் / nedil / long sound

த் / 'th' as in myth / 'dh' as in Vindhya (mountains)

த	'tha' as in Thursday	'dha' as in that
தா	'thā' as in thought	'dhā' as in dhal
தி	'thi' as in thick	'dhi' as in khaadhi
தீ	'thī' as in theme	'dhī' as in these
து	'thu' as in Thulasi	'dhu'
தூ	'thū'	'dhū'
தெ	'the'	'dhe' as in then
தே	'thē' as in Thames river	'dhē' as in they
தை	'thai' as in Thigh	'dhai' as in Thy
தொ	'tho' as in Thorax	'dho'
தோ	'thō'	'dhō' as in those
தௌ	'thau' as in thousand	'dhau' as in Thou

பயிற்சி – EXERCISES

Hierarchy of Skill Acquisition through the following exercises
I. Formation of the letter ♦ II. Correlation of sounds ♦ III. Differentiating between long and short sounds
IV. Reading words as a combination of vowels and consonants of the current series ♦ V. Series Recap

I. Learn to write by tracing the dotted lines completing each character. X = த

X	Xா	Xி	Xீ		
த	தா	தி	தீ	து	தூ
ெX	ேX	ைX	ெXா	ேXா	ெXள
தெ	தே	தை	தொ	தோ	தௌ

II. Listen to the sound of the word and write its closest equivalent Tamil letter.

THIGH - ______ THEY - ______ THE - ______

III. Fill in the missing kuril/nedil letters in this incomplete series.

த தா ______ தீ து ______

தெ ______ தை ______ தோ ______

IV. Read aloud the given words.

தாத்தா/THĀTTHĀ/ grandpa
அத்தை/ATTHAI/ aunt
ஆதி/ĀDHI/ beginning
தீ/THĪ/ fire
அது/ADHU/ that
இது/IDHU/ this
ஊது/ŪDHU/ blow
ஓது/ŌDHU/ chant
தேதி/THĒDHI/ date
உதை/UDHAI/ kick
தூது/THŪDHU/ messenger
எது / EDHU/ which

V. Fill in the letters of the 'த்' series.

த் Series = த் + (அ, ஆ, இ, ஈ, உ, ஊ, எ, ஏ, ஐ, ஒ, ஓ, ஔ)

= ___, ___, ___, ___, ___, ___, ___, ___, ___, ___, ___, ___

LESSON - பாடம்

கற்போம் வல்லினம் /KAṞPŌM VALLINAM / Let us learn Vallinam

ப் வரிசை --------------- (i)p/(i)b Series

ப் + அ = ப	(i)p + a = pa	ப் + எ = பெ	(i)p + e = pe
ப் + ஆ = பா	(i)p + ā = pā	ப் + ஏ = பே	(i)p + ē = pē
ப் + இ = பி	(i)p + i = pi	ப் + ஐ = பை	(i)p + ai = pai
ப் + ஈ = பீ	(i)p + ī = pī	ப் + ஒ = பொ	(i)p + o = po
ப் + உ = பு	(i)p + u = pu	ப் + ஓ = போ	(i)p + ō = pō
ப் + ஊ = பூ	(i)p + ū = pū	ப் + ஔ = பௌ	(i)p + au = pau

குறில் / kuril / short sound   நெடில் / nedil / long sound

ப் / 'p' as in sip / 'b' as in nib

ப	'pa'	as in pulse	/	'ba'	as in bug
பா	'pā'	as in pasta	/	'bā'	as in bark
பி	'pi'	as in pista	/	'bi'	as in bin
பீ	'pī'	as in pea	/	'bī'	as in bead
பு	'pu'	as in pull	/	'bu'	as in book
பூ	'pū'	as in pool	/	'bū'	as in boost
பெ	'pe'	as in pet	/	'be'	as in bet
பே	'pē'	as in paste	/	'bē'	as in base
பை	'pai'	as in pile	/	'bai'	as in bind
பொ	'po'	as in poet	/	'bo'	as in bovine
போ	'pō'	as in post	/	'bō'	as in boat
பௌ	'pau'	as in pound	/	'bau'	as in bowl

N.B.

The letters க, த and ப in the vallinam family are usually pronounced as **ka**, **tha** and **pa** respectively when:
(a) they are used as the first letter in the word
(b) they are preceded immediately by க, த, ப.

They are mostly pronounced as **ga**, **dha** and **ba** when they are positioned elsewhere in the word.

க் ச் ட் த் ப் ற்

பயிற்சி – EXERCISES

Hierarchy of Skill Acquisition through the following exercises
I. Formation of the letter ♦ II. Correlation of sounds ♦ III. Differentiating between long and short sounds
IV. Reading words as a combination of vowels and consonants of the current series ♦ V. Series Recap

I. Learn to write by tracing the dotted lines completing each character. X = ப

X	Xா	Xி	Xீ		
ப	பா	பி	பீ	பு	பூ
ெX	ேX	ைX	ெXா	ேXா	ெXள
பெ	பே	பை	பொ	போ	பௌ

II. Listen to the sound of the word and write its closest equivalent Tamil letter.

PIE - ☐ BYE - ☐ BEE - ☐

III. Fill in the missing kuril/nedil letters in this incomplete series.

☐	பா	பி	☐	☐	பூ
பெ	பே	☐	பொ	☐	பௌ

IV. Read aloud the given words.

அப்பா/APPĀ/ father
பாப்பா/PĀPPĀ/ child
உப்பு/UPPU/ salt
பூ/PŪ/ flower
பை/PAI/ bag
ஆப்பு/ĀPPU/ wedge (verb)
போ/PŌ/ go
ஒப்பி /OPPI/ recite

V. Fill in the letters of the 'ப்' series.

ப் Series = ப் + (அ, ஆ, இ, ஈ, உ, ஊ, எ, ஏ, ஐ, ஒ, ஓ, ஔ)

= ____, ____, ____, ____, ____, ____, ____, ____, ____, ____, ____, ____

க் ச் ட் த் ப் ற்

LESSON - பாடம்

கற்போம் வல்லினம் /KAṞPŌM VALLINAM / Let us learn Vallinam

ற் வரிசை --------------- (i)ṛ Series

ற் + அ = ற	(i)ṛ + a = ra	ற் + எ = றெ	(i) ṛ + e = re
ற் + ஆ = றா	(i) ṛ + $\bar{a}$ = r$\bar{a}$	ற் + ஏ = றே	(i) ṛ + $\bar{e}$ = r$\bar{e}$
ற் + இ = றி	(i) ṛ + i = ri	ற் + ஐ = றை	(i) ṛ + ai = ṛai
ற் + ஈ = றீ	(i) ṛ + i = r$\bar{i}$	ற் + ஒ = றொ	(i) ṛ + o = ro
ற் + உ = று	(i) ṛ + u = ṛu	ற் + ஓ = றோ	(i) ṛ + $\bar{o}$ = r$\bar{o}$
ற் + ஊ = றூ	(i) ṛ + u = r$\bar{u}$	ற் + ஔ = றௌ	(i) ṛ + au = ṛau

குறில் / kuril / short sound   நெடில் / nedil / long sound

ற் / 'ṛ' as in fur

ற	/	'ṛa'	as in	rough
றா	/	'ṛ$\bar{a}$'	as in	raw
றி	/	'ṛi'	as in	hurry
றீ	/	'ṛ$\bar{i}$'	as in	reach
று	/	'ṛu'	as in	Rudolph
றூ	/	'ṛ$\bar{u}$'	as in	roof
றெ	/	'ṛe'	as in	bread
றே	/	'ṛ$\bar{e}$'	as in	brave
றை	/	'ṛai'	as in	ripe
றொ	/	'ṛo'	as in	rotate
றோ	/	'ṛ$\bar{o}$'	as in	row
றௌ	/	'ṛau'	as in	around

N.B.

1 If 'ற்' comes right before another 'ற' in the same word, then the 'ற்' gives the sound of 't'. So read togther, 'ற்ற' gives the sound 'tR' as in "patriotic".
Example - U -t-RU/ ஊ-ற்-று

2 The difference between ற (big ra) and ர (small ra) is that you must roll the tongue back when it comes to the ற sound so that it sounds like "RR".

க் ச் ட் த் ப் ற்

பயிற்சி – EXERCISES

Hierarchy of Skill Acquisition through the following exercises
I. Formation of the letter ♦ II. Correlation of sounds ♦ III. Differentiating between long and short sounds
IV. Reading words as a combination of vowels and consonants of the current series ♦ V. Series Recap

I. Learn to write by tracing the dotted lines completing each character. X = ற

X	X‌ா	X‌ி	X‌ீ		
ற	றா	றி	றீ	று	றூ
ெX	ேX	ைX	ெXா	ேXா	ெXள
றெ	றே	றை	றொ	றோ	றௌ

II. Listen to the sound of the word and write its closest equivalent Tamil letter.

CHRISTMAS - க்_____ஸ்துமஸ்   CURRY - க____

III. Fill in the missing kuril/nedil letters in this incomplete series.

☐	றா	றி	☐	று	☐
றெ	☐	றை	றொ	☐	றௌ

IV. Read aloud the given words.

இறை/IṞAI/ divine
ஆறு/ĀṞU/river/six
அறு/AṞU/ cut
ஏறு/ĒṞU/ climb
அறை/AṞAI/ room/slap
எறி/EṞI/ throw
அறி/AṞI/ know
ஊறு/ŪṞU/ soak
உறை/UṞAI/ reside
ஈறு/ĪṞU/ gum
ஊற்று/ŪTṞU/ fountain/pour
ஆற்று/ĀTṞU/ to cool

V. Fill in the letters of the 'ற்' series.

ற் Series = ற் + (அ, ஆ, இ, ஈ, உ, ஊ, எ, ஏ, ஐ, ஒ, ஓ, ஔ)

= ____, ____, ____, ____, ____, ____, ____, ____, ____, ____, ____, ____

க் ச் ட் த் ப் ற்

RECAP : **Vallinam Family: க/ka, ச/ cha, ட/ṭa, த/tha, ப/pa, ற/ṛa**

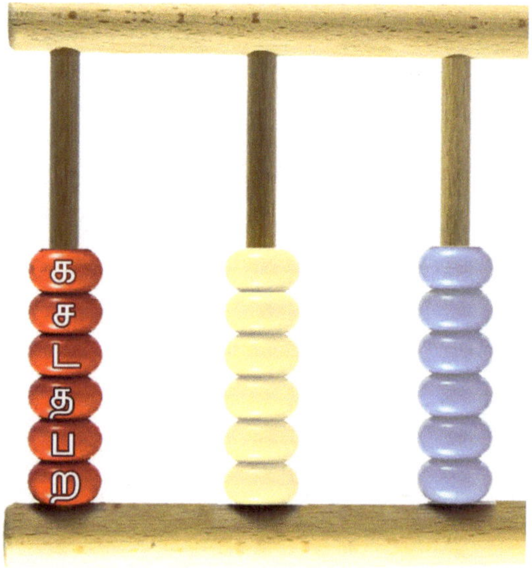

Fill in the missing letters in the table.

	அ	ஆ	இ	ஈ	உ	ஊ	எ	ஏ	ஐ	ஒ	ஓ	ஔ
க்	க		கி	கீ		கூ		கே	கை	கொ		கௌ
ச்	ச	சா		சீ	சு		செ		சை		சோ	சௌ
ட்	ட		டி		டு	டூ		டே		டொ	டோ	
த்	த	தா		தீ		தூ	தெ	தே		தொ		தௌ
ப்	ப	பா	பி	பீ	பு		பெ		பை	பொ	போ	
ற்		றா	றி	றீ		றூ	றெ	றே	றை		றோ	றௌ

Now you will be able to read the Tamil names for a few numbers, colours and parts of the body once you have understood how to read the 12 vowels and the Vallinam family of consonants! Try reading the Tamil words below.

I Colours : purple / ஊதா green / பச்சை

II Numbers : 6/ஆறு 8/எட்டு 10/பத்து

III Body Parts : ear / காது hand / கை

Able to read?

If 'Yes', Congratulations ! Keep it up!

If 'No', Congratulations ! Keep trying, because those who said 'Yes' now, have tried lot of times earlier, only then succeeded!

So you are on the RIGHT TRACK! All The Best !

ACTIVITY - I

I. Write out the names of these colors in Tamil.

II. Write out the numbers of objects in Tamil.

III. Write out the names of parts of the body as indicated in Tamil.

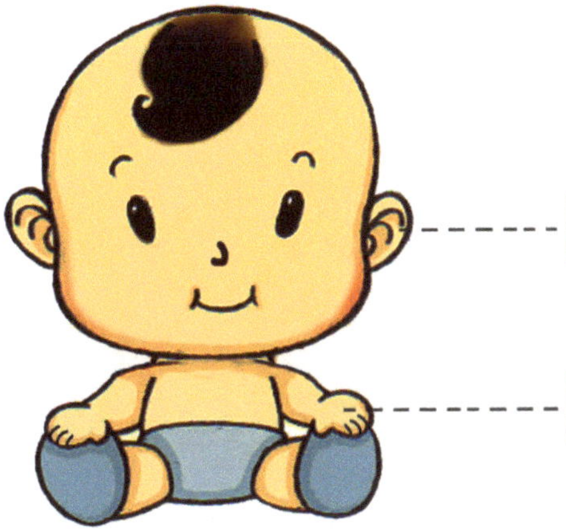

LESSON - பாடம்

கற்போம் இடையினம்/KAṚPŌM IḌAIYIN̲AM / Let us learn Idaiyinam

ய் வரிசை --------------- (i)y Series

ய் + அ = ய	(i)y + a = ya	ய் + எ = யெ	(i)y + e = ye
ய் + ஆ = யா	(i)y + ā = yā	ய் + ஏ = யே	(i)y + ē = yē
ய் + இ = யி	(i)y + i = yi	ய் + ஐ = யை	(i)y + ai = yai
ய் + ஈ = யீ	(i)y + ī = yī	ய் + ஒ = யொ	(i)y + o = yo
ய் + உ = யு	(i)y + u = yu	ய் + ஓ = யோ	(i)y + ō = yō
ய் + ஊ = யூ	(i)y + ū = yū	ய் + ஔ = யௌ	(i)y + au = yau

குறில் /kuril / short sound   நெடில் /nedil / long sound

ய்
ர்
ல்
வ்
ழ்
ள்

ய் / 'y' as in sail

ய	/	'ya'	as in	violin
யா	/	'yā'	as in	yard
யி	/	'yi'	as in	yin-yang
யீ	/	'yī'	as in	yeast
யு	/	'yu'	as in	unique
யூ	/	'yū'	as in	youth
யெ	/	'ye'	as in	yellow
யே	/	'yē'	as in	Yale (University)
யை	/	'yai'	as in	yikes
யொ	/		'yo'	
யோ	/	'yō'	as in	yolk
யௌ	/		'yau'	

பயிற்சி – EXERCISES

Hierarchy of Skill Acquisition through the following exercises
I. Formation of the letter ♦ II. Correlation of sounds ♦ III. Differentiating between long and short sounds ♦ IV. Reading words as a combination of vowels and consonants of the current series ♦ V. Series Recap

I. Learn to write by tracing the dotted lines completing each character. X = ய

X	Xா	Xி	Xீ		
ய	யா	யி	யீ	யு	யூ
ெX	ேX	ைX	ொX	ோX	ௌX
யெ	யே	யை	யொ	யோ	யௌ

II. Listen to the sound of the word and write its closest equivalent Tamil letter.

YOU - ____ YO-YO - ____

III. Fill in the missing kuril/nedil letters in this incomplete series.

ய ____ யி யீ ____ யூ

____ யே ____ யொ யோ ____

IV. Read aloud the given words.

ஆயா/$\bar{A}$Y$\bar{A}$/ grandmother

ஐயா/அய்யா/AIYY$\bar{A}$/ Respectful address for a man (Sir)

V. Fill in the letters of the 'ய்' series.

ய் Series = ய் + (அ, ஆ, இ, ஈ, உ, ஊ, எ, ஏ, ஐ, ஒ, ஓ, ஔ)

= ___, ___, ___, ___, ___, ___, ___, ___, ___, ___, ___, ___

LESSON - பாடம்

கற்போம் இடையினம் / KAṞPŌM IḌAIYIṈAM / Let us learn Idaiyinam

ர் வரிசை --------------- (i)r Series

ர் + அ = ர	(i)r + a = ra	ர் + எ = ரெ	(i)r + e = re
ர் + ஆ = ரா	(i)r + $\bar{a}$ = r$\bar{a}$	ர் + ஏ = ரே	(i)r + $\bar{e}$ = r$\bar{e}$
ர் + இ = ரி	(i)r + I = ri	ர் + ஐ = ரை	(i)r + ai = rai
ர் + ஈ = ரீ	(i)r + $\bar{\imath}$ = r$\bar{\imath}$	ர் + ஒ = ரொ	(i)r + o = ro
ர் + உ = ரு	(i)r + u = ru	ர் + ஓ = ரோ	(i)r + $\bar{o}$ = r$\bar{o}$
ர் + ஊ = ரூ	(i)r + $\bar{u}$ = r$\bar{u}$	ர் + ஔ = ரௌ	(i)r + au = rau

குறில் /kuril / short sound   நெடில் /nedil / long sound

ர் / 'r' as in sir

ர	/	'ra'	as in	run
ரா	/	'r$\bar{a}$'	as in	rod
ரி	/	'ri'	as in	river
ரீ	/	'r$\bar{\imath}$'	as in	reason
ரு	/	'ru'	as in	rupee
ரூ	/	'r$\bar{u}$'	as in	room
ரெ	/	're'	as in	red
ரே	/	'r$\bar{e}$'	as in	range
ரை	/	'rai'	as in	rise
ரொ	/	'ro'	as in	Romania
ரோ	/	'r$\bar{o}$'	as in	rose
ரௌ	/	'rau'	as in	round

ய் ர் ல் வ் ழ் ள்

பயிற்சி - EXERCISES

Hierarchy of Skill Acquisition through the following exercises
I. Formation of the letter ♦ II. Correlation of sounds ♦ III. Differentiating between long and short sounds
IV. Reading words as a combination of vowels and consonants of the current series ♦ V. Series Recap

I. Learn to write by tracing the dotted lines completing each character. X= ர

X	Xா	Xி	Xீ		
ர	ரா	ரி	ரீ	ரு	ரூ
ெX	ேX	ைX	ெXா	ேXா	ெXள
ரெ	ரே	ரை	ரொ	ரோ	ரௌ

II. Listen to the sound of the word and write its closest equivalent Tamil letter.

RAY - ☐ RAW - ☐ ROW - ☐

III. Fill in the missing kuril/nedil letters in this incomplete series.

ர ☐ ரி ரீ ☐ ரூ

☐ ரே ☐ ரொ ரோ ☐

IV. Read aloud the given words.

அரி/ARI/ cut	அரை/ARAI/ grind	இரு/IRU/ stay
இரை/IRAI/prey	உரி/URI/ peel	ஊர்/ŪR/ town

V. Fill in the letters of the 'ர்' series.

ர் Series = ர் + (அ, ஆ, இ, ஈ, உ, ஊ, எ, ஏ, ஐ, ஒ, ஓ, ஔ)

= ____,____,____,____,____,____,____,____,____,____,____,____

LESSON - பாடம்

கற்போம் இடையினம் / KAṞPŌM IḌAI YIṈAM / Let us learn Idaiyinam

ல் வரிசை --------------- (i)l Series

ல் + அ = ல	(i)l + a = la	ல் + எ = லெ	(i)l + e = le
ல் + ஆ = லா	(i)l + $\bar{a}$ = l$\bar{a}$	ல் + ஏ = லே	(i)l + $\bar{e}$ = l$\bar{e}$
ல் + இ = லி	(i)l + i = li	ல் + ஐ = லை	(i)l + ai = lai
ல் + ஈ = லீ	(i)l + $\bar{\imath}$ = l$\bar{\imath}$	ல் + ஒ = லொ	(i)l + o = lo
ல் + உ = லு	(i)l + u = lu	ல் + ஓ = லோ	(i)l + $\bar{o}$ = l$\bar{o}$
ல் + ஊ = லூ	(i)l + $\bar{u}$ = l$\bar{u}$	ல் + ஔ = லௌ	(i)l + au = lau

குறில் / kuril / short sound   நெடில் / nedil / long sound

ல் / 'l' as in bill

ல	/	'la'	as in	love
லா	/	'l$\bar{a}$'	as in	lawn
லி	/	'li'	as in	list
லீ	/	'l$\bar{\imath}$'	as in	leave
லு	/	'lu'	as in	look
லூ	/	'l$\bar{u}$'	as in	loop
லெ	/	'le'	as in	less
லே	/	'l$\bar{e}$'	as in	lake
லை	/	'lai'	as in	line
லொ	/	'lo'	as in	Colombo
லோ	/	'l$\bar{o}$'	as in	load
லௌ	/	'lau''	as in	loud

ய் ர் ல் வ் ழ் ள்

பயிற்சி - EXERCISES

Hierarchy of Skill Acquisition through the following exercises
I. Formation of the letter ♦ II. Correlation of sounds ♦ III. Differentiating between long and short sounds
IV. Reading words as a combination of vowels and consonants of the current series ♦ V. Series Recap

I. Learn to write by tracing the dotted lines completing each character. X = ல

X	Xா	Xி	Xீ		
ல	லா	லி	லீ	லு	லூ
ெX	ேX	ைX	ெXா	ேXா	ெXள
லெ	லே	லை	லொ	லோ	லௌ

II. Listen to the sound of the word and write its closest equivalent Tamil letter.

LAW - ☐ LOW - ☐ LAY - ☐

III. Fill in the missing kuril/nedil letters in this incomplete series.

ல ☐ ☐ லீ ☐ லூ

லெ லே லை ☐ லோ ☐

IV. Read aloud the given words.

அலை/ALAI/ wave
ஆலை/ĀLAI/ factory
இலை/ILAI/ leaf
ஒல்லி/OLLI/ thin
இல்லை/ILLAI/ no/not
ஒலி/OLI/ sound
எலி/ELI/ rat
ஓலை/ŌLAI/ parchment
உலா/ULĀ/ go around

V. Fill in the letters of the 'ல்' series.

ல் Series = ல் + (அ, ஆ, இ, ஈ, உ, ஊ, எ, ஏ, ஐ, ஒ, ஓ, ஔ)

= ____,____,____,____,____,____,____,____,____,____,____,____

LESSON - பாடம்

கற்போம் இடையினம்/KAṞPŌM IḌAIYIṈAM / Let us learn Idaiyinam

வ் வரிசை --------------- (i)v Series

வ் + அ = வ	(i)v + a = va	வ் + எ = வெ	(i)v + e = ve
வ் + ஆ = வா	(i)v + $\bar{a}$ = v$\bar{a}$	வ் + ஏ = வே	(i)v + $\bar{e}$ = v$\bar{e}$
வ் + இ = வி	(i)v + i = vi	வ் + ஐ = வை	(i)v + ai = vai
வ் + ஈ = வீ	(i)v + $\bar{\imath}$ = v$\bar{\imath}$	வ் + ஒ = வொ	(i)v + o = vo
வ் + உ = வு	(i)v + u = vu	வ் + ஓ = வோ	(i)v + $\bar{o}$ = v$\bar{o}$
வ் + ஊ = வூ	(i)v + $\bar{u}$ = v$\bar{u}$	வ் + ஔ = வெள	(i)v + au = vau

குறில்/ kuril / short sound   நெடில் / nedil / long sound

வ் / 'v' as in give

வ	/	'va'	as in	cover
வா	/	'v$\bar{a}$'	as in	volume
வி	/	'vi'	as in	villain
வீ	/	'v$\bar{\imath}$'	as in	wheel
வு	/	'vu'	as in	wood
வூ	/	'v$\bar{u}$'	as in	wound
வெ	/	've'	as in	vent
வே	/	'v$\bar{e}$'	as in	vacant
வை	/	'vai'	as in	vine
வொ	/	'vo'	as in	vocabulary
வோ	/	'v$\bar{o}$'	as in	vote
வெள	/	'vou'	as in	voucher

N.B.
To represent English sounds "w" and "v", only one Tamil letter is used and its sound is the same as "v".

All examples spelled with the letter "w" should be read out with the "v" sound.

ய் ர் ல் வ் ழ் ள்

பயிற்சி – EXERCISES

Hierarchy of Skill Acquisition through the following exercises
I. Formation of the letter ♦ II. Correlation of sounds ♦ III. Differentiating between long and short sounds
IV. Reading words as a combination of vowels and consonants of the current series ♦ V. Series Recap

I. Learn to write by tracing the dotted lines completing each character. X = வ

X	Xா	Xி	Xீ		
வ	வா	வி	வீ	வு	வூ
ெX	ேX	ைX	ெXா	ேXா	ெXள
வெ	வே	வை	வொ	வோ	வௌ

II. Listen to the sound of the word and write its closest equivalent Tamil letter.

WAY - ____ WE - ____ WHY - ____

III. Fill in the missing kuril/nedil letters in this incomplete series.

____	வா	வி	____	வு	____
வெ	____	வை	வொ	____	வௌ

IV. Read aloud the given words.

அவை/AVAI/court/those **வேவு**/V$\bar{E}$VU/ spying **வா**/V$\bar{A}$/ come
ஆவி/$\bar{A}$VI/ steam **ஏவு**/$\bar{E}$VU/ order **ஔவை**/AUVAI/ Auvai
இவை/IVAI/these **அவா**/AV$\bar{A}$/ desire **எவை**/EVAI/which ones

V. Fill in the letters of the 'வ்' series.

வ் Series = வ் + (அ, ஆ, இ, ஈ, உ, ஊ, எ, ஏ, ஐ, ஒ, ஓ, ஔ)

= ____, ____, ____, ____, ____, ____, ____, ____, ____, ____, ____, ____

LESSON - பாடம்

கற்போம் இடையினம்/KAṞPŌM IḌAIYIṈAM / Let us learn Idaiyinam

ழ் வரிசை --------------- (i)zh Series

ழ்	+	அ	=	ழ	(i)zh + a = zha	ழ்	+	எ	=	ழெ (i)zh + e = zhe
ழ்	+	ஆ	=	ழா	(i)zh + $\bar{a}$ = zh$\bar{a}$	ழ்	+	ஏ	=	ழே (i)zh + $\bar{e}$ = zh$\bar{e}$
ழ்	+	இ	=	ழி	(i)zh + i = zhi	ழ்	+	ஐ	=	ழை (i)zh + ai = zhai
ழ்	+	ஈ	=	ழீ	(i)zh + $\bar{i}$ = zh$\bar{i}$	ழ்	+	ஒ	=	ழொ (i)zh + o = zho
ழ்	+	உ	=	ழு	(i)zh + u = zhu	ழ்	+	ஓ	=	ழோ (i)zh + $\bar{o}$ = zh$\bar{o}$
ழ்	+	ஊ	=	ழூ	(i)zh + $\bar{u}$ = zh$\bar{u}$	ழ்	+	ஔ	=	ழௌ (i)zh + au = zhau

குறில்/kuril / short sound   நெடில் /nedil / long sound

ழ் / 'zh' as in Thamizh

ழ	/	'zha'	as in	அழகு	(azhagu)
ழா	/	'zh$\bar{a}$'	as in	குழாய்	(kuzh$\bar{a}$y)
ழி	/	'zhi'	as in	ஆழி	($\bar{a}$zhi)
ழீ	/	'zh$\bar{i}$'	as in	வாழீ	(v$\bar{a}$zh$\bar{i}$)
ழு	/	'zhu'	as in	கழுதை	(kazhuthai)
ழூ	/	'zh$\bar{u}$'	as in	புகழூர்	(Pugazhur)
ழெ	/	'zhe'	as in	புகழெட்டு	(Pugazheṭṭu)
ழே	/	'zh$\bar{e}$'	as in	இகழேல்	(igazh$\bar{e}$l)
ழை	/	'zhai'	as in	வாழை	(v$\bar{a}$zhai)
ழொ	/		'zho'		
ழோ	/	'zh$\bar{o}$'	as in	யாழோசை	(y$\bar{a}$zh$\bar{o}$sai)
ழௌ	/		'zhau'		

N.B.

"ழ" has a unique pronunciation in Tamil. There is no word or combination of letters in English to indicate the equivalent or similar sound to 'zh'. Therefore, one can learn its usage only through Tamil words.

பயிற்சி - EXERCISES

Hierarchy of Skill Acquisition through the following exercises
I. Formation of the letter ♦ II. Correlation of sounds ♦ III. Differentiating between long and short sounds
IV. Reading words as a combination of vowels and consonants of the current series ♦ V. Series Recap

I. Learn to write by tracing the dotted lines completing each character. X = ழ

X	Xா	Xி	Xீ		
ழ	ழா	ழி	ழீ	ழு	ழூ
ெX	ேX	ைX	ெXா	ேXா	ெXள
ழெ	ழே	ழை	ழொ	ழோ	ழௌ

II. Listen to the sound of the word and write its closest equivalent Tamil letter.

YĀZH - யா____ THAMIZH - தமி____

III. Fill in the missing kuril/nedil letters in this incomplete series.

☐	ழா	☐	ழீ	ழு	ழூ
ழெ	☐	☐	ழொ	ழோ	☐

IV. Read aloud the given words.

இழை/IZHAI/ thread
உழை/UZHAI/ work
ஆழி/ĀZHI/sea
அழி/AZHI/ erase
இழு/IZHU/ pull
உழு/UZHU/plough
அழை/AZHAI/ invite
எழு/EZHU/get up
ஏழு/ĒZHU/seven
ஊழ்/ŪZH/previous

V. Fill in the letters of the 'ழ்' series.

ழ் Series = ழ் + (அ, ஆ, இ, ஈ, உ, ஊ, எ, ஏ, ஐ, ஒ, ஓ, ஔ)

= ____, ____, ____, ____, ____, ____, ____, ____, ____, ____, ____, ____

LESSON - பாடம்

கற்போம் இடையினம் / KAṞPŌM IḌAIYIṈAM / Let us learn Idaiyinam

ள் வரிசை --------------- '(i)ḷ' Series

ள் + அ = ள	(i)ḷ + a = ḷa	ள் + எ = ளெ	(i)ḷ + e = ḷe
ள் + ஆ = ளா	(i)ḷ + ā = ḷā	ள் + ஏ = ளே	(i)ḷ + ē = ḷē
ள் + இ = ளி	(i)ḷ + i = ḷi	ள் + ஐ = ளை	(i)ḷ + ai = ḷai
ள் + ஈ = ளீ	(i)ḷ + ī = ḷī	ள் + ஒ = ளொ	(i)ḷ + o = ḷo
ள் + உ = ளு	(i)ḷ + u = ḷu	ள் + ஓ = ளோ	(i)ḷ + ō = ḷō
ள் + ஊ = ளூ	(i)ḷ + ū = ḷū	ள் + ஔ = ளௌ	(i)ḷ + au = ḷau

குறில் / kuril / short sound   நெடில் / nedil / long sound

ள் / 'ḷ' as in girl

ள	/	'ḷa'	as in	plum
ளா	/	'ḷā'	as in	floss
ளி	/	'ḷi'	as in	cling
ளீ	/	'ḷī'	as in	clean
ளு	/	'ḷu'	as in	Thulu language
ளூ	/	'ḷū'	as in	blue
ளெ	/	'ḷe'	as in	blender
ளே	/	'ḷē'	as in	play
ளை	/	'ḷai'	as in	flight
ளொ	/	'ḷo'		
ளோ	/	'ḷō'	as in	glow
ளௌ	/	'ḷau'	as in	clown

N.B.

The difference between ள (big la) and ல (small la) is that you must roll the tongue back when it comes to 'ள' to emphasize the sound of 'LL'.

பயிற்சி - EXERCISES

Hierarchy of Skill Acquisition through the following exercises
I. Formation of the letter ♦ II. Correlation of sounds ♦ III. Differentiating between long and short sounds
IV. Reading words as a combination of vowels and consonants of the current series ♦ V. Series Recap

I. Learn to write by tracing the dotted lines completing each character. X = ள

X	Xா	Xி	Xீ		
ள	ளா	ளி	ளீ	ளு	ளூ
ெX	ேX	ைX	ெXா	ேXா	ெXள
ளெ	ளே	ளை	ளொ	ளோ	ளௌ

II. Listen to the sound of the word and write its closest equivalent Tamil letter.

GLUE - க்

BLOW - ப்

III. Fill in the missing kuril/nedil letters in this incomplete series.

☐	ளா	☐	ளீ	ளு	☐
ளெ	☐	ளை	☐	ளோ	ளௌ

IV. Read aloud the given words.

இளி/IḶI/ smile widely
ஒளி/OḶI/ light
உளி/UḶI/ hammer
அள்ளு/AḶḶU/ collect
உள்ளே/UḶḶĒ/ inside
ஆள்/ĀḶ/ person
ஊளை/ŪḶAI/ howl
எள்/EḶ/ sesame

V. Fill in the letters of the 'ள்' series.

ள் Series = ள் + (அ, ஆ, இ, ஈ, உ, ஊ, எ, ஏ, ஐ, ஒ, ஓ, ஔ)

= ____, ____, ____, ____, ____, ____, ____, ____, ____, ____, ____, ____

RECAP : **Idaiyinam Family: ய/ya, ர/ra, ல/la, வ/va, ழ/zha, ள/ḷa**

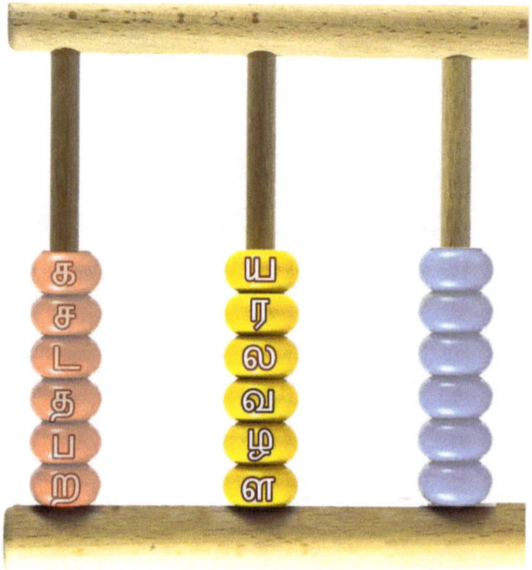

Fill in the missing letters in the table.

	அ	ஆ	இ	ஈ	உ	ஊ	எ	ஏ	ஐ	ஒ	ஓ	ஔ
ய்	ய	யா		யீ		யூ		யே	யை		யோ	யௌ
ர்	ர		ரி	ரீ		ரூ	ரெ		ரை	ரொ	ரோ	
ல்	ல	லா		லீ	லு		லெ	லே		லொ		லௌ
வ்	வ	வா	வி		வு	வூ	வெ		வை	வொ	வோ	வௌ
ழ்	ழ		ழி	ழீ	ழு		ழெ	ழே	ழை		ழோ	ழௌ
ள்	ள		ளி		ளு	ளூ		ளே		ளொ	ளோ	

Now you know how to read the 12 vowels, the Vallinam and the Idaiyinam family of consonants!
Try reading the Tamil words below.

I Colours : white/வெள்ளை black/கருப்பு red/சிவப்பு

II Numbers : 7/ஏழு

III Body Parts : mouth/வாய் finger/விரல் leg/கால்
head/தலை stomach/வயிறு neck/கழுத்து

ACTIVITY - II

I. Write out the names of these colors in Tamil.

II. Write out the numbers of objects in Tamil.

III. Write out the names of parts of the body as indicated in Tamil.

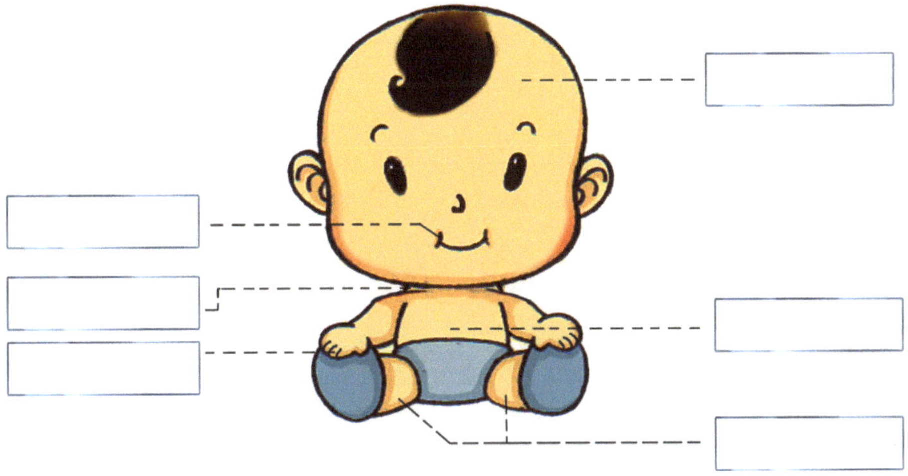

LESSON - பாடம்

கற்போம் மெல்லினம் / KAṞPŌM MELLIṈAM / Let us learn Mellinam

ங் வரிசை --------------- '(i)ṅ' Series

ங் + அ = ங	(i)ṅ + a = ṅa	ங் + எ = ஙெ	(i)ṅ + e = ṅe
ங் + ஆ = ஙா	(i)ṅ + ā = ṅā	ங் + ஏ = ஙே	(i)ṅ + ē = ṅē
ங் + இ = ஙி	(i)ṅ + i = ṅi	ங் + ஐ = ஙை	(i)ṅ + ai = ṅai
ங் + ஈ = ஙீ	(i)ṅ + ī = ṅī	ங் + ஒ = ஙொ	(i)ṅ + o = ṅo
ங் + உ = ஙு	(i)ṅ + u = ṅu	ங் + ஓ = ஙோ	(i)ṅ + ō = ṅō
ங் + ஊ = ஙூ	(i)ṅ + ū = ṅū	ங் + ஔ = ஙௌ	(i)ṅ + au = ṅau

குறில் / kuril / short sound   நெடில் / nedil / long sound

ங் / '(i)ṅ' as in 'English'

ங்க	/	'ṅga'	as in	finger
ங்கா	/	'ṅgā'	as in	Bengal
ங்கி	/	'ṅgi'	as in	swinging
ங்கீ	/	'ṅgī'	as in	tangy
ங்கு	/	'ṅgu'	as in	dengue
ங்கூ	/	'ṅgū'	as in	mongoose
ங்கெ	/	'ṅge'		
ங்கே	/	'ṅgē'	as in	engage
ங்கை	/	'ṅgai'	as in	fungi
ங்கொ	/	'ṅgo'		
ங்கோ	/	'ṅgō'	as in	mango
ங்கௌ	/	'ṅgau'	as in	hangout

These consonants of the ங் family are no longer used in today's written and spoken Thamizh. Our usage has now been constricted to using only "ங்" in combination with the "க்" group (as shown on the side) to produce the "ng" sound.

பயிற்சி – EXERCISES

Hierarchy of Skill Acquisition through the following exercises
I. Formation of the letter ♦ II. Correlation of sounds ♦ III. Differentiating between long and short sounds
IV. Reading words as a combination of vowels and consonants of the current series ♦ V. Series Recap

I. Learn to write by tracing the dotted lines completing each character. X = ங

X	Xா	Xி	Xீ		
ங	ஙா	ஙி	ஙீ	ஙு	ஙூ
ெX	ேX	ைX	ெXா	ேXா	ெXள
ஙெ	ஙே	ஙை	ஙொ	ஙோ	ஙௌ

II. Listen to the sound of the word and write its closest equivalent Tamil letter.

SONG - சா___ WRONG - ரா___

III. Fill in the missing kuril/nedil letters in this incomplete series.

☐ ஙா ☐ ஙீ ஙு ☐

ஙெ ☐ ஙை ☐ ஙோ ஙௌ

IV. Read aloud the given words.

சங்கம் /SANGAM/ club
அங்கம் /ANGAM/ part
சிங்கம் /SINGAM/ lion
எங்கு /ENGU/ where
அங்கு /ANGU/ there
இங்கு /INGU/ here
எங்கு /ENGU/ where
ஆங்கிலம்/ĀNGILAM/English
மாங்காய்/MĀNGĀI/raw mango

V. Fill in the letters of the 'ங்' series.

ங் Series = ங் + (அ, ஆ, இ, ஈ, உ, ஊ, எ, ஏ, ஐ, ஒ, ஓ, ஔ)

= ___, ___, ___, ___, ___, ___, ___, ___, ___, ___, ___, ___

LESSON - பாடம்

கற்போம் மெல்லினம் / KAṞPŌM MELLIṈAM / Let us learn Mellinam

ஞ் வரிசை -------------- '(i)ñ' Series

ஞ் + அ = ஞ	(i)ñ + a = ña	ஞ் + எ = ஞெ	(i)ñ + e = ñe
ஞ் + ஆ = ஞா	(i)ñ + ā = ñā	ஞ் + ஏ = ஞே	(i)ñ + ē = ñē
ஞ் + இ = ஞி	(i)ñ + i = ñi	ஞ் + ஐ = ஞை	(i)ñ + ai = ñai
ஞ் + ஈ = ஞீ	(i)ñ + ī = ñī	ஞ் + ஒ = ஞொ	(i)ñ + o = ño
ஞ் + உ = ஞு	(i)ñ + u = ñu	ஞ் + ஓ = ஞோ	(i)ñ + ō = ñō
ஞ் + ஊ = ஞூ	(i)ñ + ū = ñū	ஞ் + ஔ = ஞௌ	(i)ñ + au = ñau

குறில் / kuril / short sound   நெடில் / nedil / long sound

ஞ் / (i)ñ as in 'orange'/'syringe'

English Equivalents are not mentioned here because the nuance in differentiating between pronouncing 'ñ' and 'n' does not exist in English words. Also, different letters would be used to spell the same English word in Thamizh. This causes confusion at early stages of learning and hence will not be dealt in depth.

The sound of "ஞ" can vary in accordance with the following rules:

Rule 1: The letter "ஞ்" , when not followed by any other letter of the "ஞ" series, or when followed by any letter of the "ச" house, is pronounced as "(i)nj".
Example: (i)nj as in Injection, Ginger

Rule 2: Any letter from the "ஞ்" house except "ஞ்" itself is pronounced as "(i)nyh".
Example: Banyan, Onion

When saying "nyh", the tip of the tongue must not touch the roof of the mouth (as we generally tend to do when enunciating the "n"). Try making the "nyh" sound with the tip of your tongue touching the floor of your mouth.

பயிற்சி – EXERCISES

Hierarchy of Skill Acquisition through the following exercises
I. Formation of the letter ♦ II. Correlation of sounds ♦ III. Differentiating between long and short sounds
IV. Reading words as a combination of vowels and consonants of the current series ♦ V. Series Recap

I. Learn to write by tracing the dotted lines completing each character. X = ஞ

X	Xா	Xி	Xீ		
ஞ	ஞா	ஞி	ஞீ	ஞு	ஞூ
ெX	ேX	ைX	ெXா	ேXா	ெXள
ஞெ	ஞே	ஞை	ஞொ	ஞோ	ஞௌ

II. Listen to the sound of the word and write its closest equivalent Tamil letter.

ANGEL - ஏ_____சல் RANGE - ரே_____ச்

III. Fill in the missing kuril/nedil letters in this incomplete series.

ஞ	☐	☐	ஞீ	☐	ஞூ
ஞெ	ஞே	ஞை	ஞொ	☐	☐

IV. Read aloud the given words.

மெய்ஞ்ஞானம்/MEIÑÑĀN̲AM/ True knowledge
அஞ்ஞானம்/AÑÑĀN̲AM/ false knowledge
விஞ்ஞானம்/VIÑĀN̲AM/ science
ஞாயிறு/ÑĀYIRU/sun/sunday
ஞாபகம்/ÑĀPAGAM/ remember
கொஞ்சம்/KONJAM/ little
பஞ்சு/PANJU/ cotton
ஊஞ்சல்/ŪNJAL/ swing
இஞ்சி/INJI/ ginger
மஞ்சள்/MANJAḶ/ yellow/turmeric

V. Fill in the letters of the 'ஞ்' series.

ஞ் Series = ஞ் + (அ, ஆ, இ, ஈ, உ, ஊ, எ, ஏ, ஐ, ஒ, ஓ, ஔ)

= ____,____,____,____,____,____,____,____,____,____,____,____

LESSON - பாடம்

கற்போம் மெல்லினம் / KAṞPŌM MELLIṈAM / Let us learn Mellinam

ண் வரிசை ------------- '(i)ṇ' Series

ண் + அ = ண	(i)ṇ + a = ṇa	ண் + எ = ணெ	(i)ṇ + e = ṇe
ண் + ஆ = ணா	(i)ṇ + ā = ṇā	ண் + ஏ = ணே	(i)ṇ + ē = ṇē
ண் + இ = ணி	(i)ṇ + i = ṇi	ண் + ஐ = ணை	(i)ṇ + ai = ṇai
ண் + ஈ = ணீ	(i)ṇ + ī = ṇī	ண் + ஒ = ணொ	(i)ṇ + o = ṇo
ண் + உ = ணு	(i)ṇ + u = ṇu	ண் + ஓ = ணோ	(i)ṇ + ō = ṇō
ண் + ஊ = ணூ	(i)ṇ + ū = ṇū	ண் + ஔ = ணௌ	(i)ṇ + au = ṇau

குறில் / kuril / short sound   நெடில் / nedil / long sound

ண்	/	'ṇ'	as in	tin
ண	/	'ṇa'	as in	winner
ணா	/	'ṇā'	as in	knot
ணி	/	'ṇi'	as in	many
ணீ	/	'ṇī'	as in	knee
ணு	/	'ṇu'	as in	nook
ணூ	/	'ṇū'	as in	snoop
ணெ	/	'ṇe'	as in	neck
ணே	/	'ṇē'	as in	name
ணை	/	'ṇai'	as in	knife
ணொ	/	'ṇo'	as in	annotation
ணோ	/	'ṇō'	as in	nose
ணௌ	/	'ṇau'	as in	snout

N.B.

The difference between 'ண' (3 circled na) and 'ன', 'ந' (2 circled na, small na) is that you must roll the tongue backwards when it comes to ண to emphasize its sound.

ங் ஞ் ண் ந் ம் ன்

பயிற்சி – EXERCISES

Hierarchy of Skill Acquisition through the following exercises

I. Formation of the letter ♦ II. Correlation of sounds ♦ III. Differentiating between long and short sounds

IV. Reading words as a combination of vowels and consonants of the current series ♦ V. Series Recap

I. Learn to write by tracing the dotted lines completing each character. X = ண

X	Xா	Xி	Xீ		
ண	ணா	ணி	ணீ	ணு	ணூ
ெX	ேX	ைX	ொX	ோX	ௌX
ணெ	ணே	ணை	ணொ	ணோ	ணௌ

II. Listen to the sound of the word and write its closest equivalent Tamil letter.

MONEY - ம

III. Fill in the missing kuril/nedil letters in this incomplete series.

ண		ணி	ணீ		
ணெ	ணே			ணோ	ணௌ

IV. Read aloud the given words.

அணை/ANAI/ dam

எண்/EN/ number/count

அண்ணா/ANNĀ/elder brother

அண்ணி/ANNI/ big brother's wife

அணு/ANU/ atom

ஆண்/ĀN/ male

ஆணி/ ĀNI/ screw

இணை/INAI/ join

ஏணி/ ĒNI/ ladder

அணி/ANI/ team/wear

உண்/UN/ eat

ஆணை/ĀNAI/ order

V. Fill in the letters of the 'ண்' series.

ண் Series = ண் + (அ, ஆ, இ, ஈ, உ, ஊ, எ, ஏ, ஐ, ஒ, ஓ, ஔ)

= ____, ____, ____, ____, ____, ____, ____, ____, ____, ____, ____, ____

LESSON - பாடம்

கற்போம் மெல்லினம் / KAṞPŌM MELLIṈAM / Let us learn Mellinam

ந் வரிசை --------------- '(i)n' Series

ந் + அ = ந	(i)n + a = na	ந் + எ = நெ	(i)n + e = ne
ந் + ஆ = நா	(i)n + $\bar{a}$ = n$\bar{a}$	ந் + ஏ = நே	(i)n + $\bar{e}$ = n$\bar{e}$
ந் + இ = நி	(i)n + i = ni	ந் + ஐ = நை	(i)n + ai = nai
ந் + ஈ = நீ	(i)n + $\bar{\imath}$ = n$\bar{\imath}$	ந் + ஒ = நொ	(i)n + o = no
ந் + உ = நு	(i)n + u = nu	ந் + ஓ = நோ	(i)n + $\bar{o}$ = n$\bar{o}$
ந் + ஊ = நூ	(i)n + $\bar{u}$ = n$\bar{u}$	ந் + ஔ = நௌ	(i)n + au = nau

குறில் / kuril / short sound   நெடில் / nedil / long sound

ந்	/	'n'	as in	India
ந	/	'na'	as in	nut
நா	/	'n$\bar{a}$'	as in	nod
நி	/	'ni'	as in	nickel
நீ	/	'n$\bar{\imath}$'	as in	neat
நு	/	'nu'	as in	Anupam
நூ	/	'n$\bar{u}$'	as in	Noodles
நெ	/	'ne'	as in	nest
நே	/	'n$\bar{e}$'	as in	nape
நை	/	'nai'	as in	Nile
நொ	/	'no'	as in	Noida
நோ	/	'n$\bar{o}$'	as in	Note
நௌ	/	'nau'	as in	noun

ங் ஞ் ண் ந் ம் ன்

பயிற்சி – EXERCISES

Hierarchy of Skill Acquisition through the following exercises
I. Formation of the letter ♦ II. Correlation of sounds ♦ III. Differentiating between long and short sounds
IV. Reading words as a combination of vowels and consonants of the current series ♦ V. Series Recap

I. Learn to write by tracing the dotted lines completing each character. X = ந

X	Xா	Xி	Xீ		
ந	நா	நி	நீ	நு	நூ
ெX	ேX	ைX	ெXா	ேXா	ெXள
நெ	நே	நை	நொ	நோ	நௌ

II. Listen to the sound of the word and write its closest equivalent Tamil letter.

NO -- ☐ NOW -- ☐

III. Fill in the missing kuril/nedil letters in this incomplete series.

ந	நா	☐	நீ	☐	நூ
☐	நே	☐	நொ	நோ	☐

IV. Read aloud the given words.

நீ/ Nī/you

V. Fill in the letters of the 'ந்' series.

ந் Series = ந் + (அ, ஆ, இ, ஈ, உ, ஊ, எ, ஏ, ஐ, ஒ, ஓ, ஔ)

= ____,____,____,____,____,____,____,____,____,____,____,____

ங் ஞ் ண் ந் ம் ன்

LESSON - பாடம்

கற்போம் மெல்லினம் / KARPŌM MELLINAM / Let us learn Mellinam

ம் வரிசை -------------- '(i)m' Series

ம் + அ = ம	(i)m + a =	ma		ம் + எ = மெ	(i)m + e =	me
ம் + ஆ = மா	(i)m + $\bar{a}$ =	m$\bar{a}$		ம் + ஏ = மே	(i)m + $\bar{e}$ =	m$\bar{e}$
ம் + இ = மி	(i)m + i =	mi		ம் + ஐ = மை	(i)m + ai =	mai
ம் + ஈ = மீ	(i)m + $\bar{\imath}$ =	m$\bar{\imath}$		ம் + ஒ = மொ	(i)m + o =	mo
ம் + உ = மு	(i)m + u =	mu		ம் + ஓ = மோ	(i)m + $\bar{o}$ =	m$\bar{o}$
ம் + ஊ = மூ	(i)m + $\bar{u}$ =	m$\bar{u}$		ம் + ஔ = மௌ	(i)m + au =	mau

குறில் / kuril / short sound   நெடில் / nedil / long sound

ம்	/	'(i)m'	as in	grim
ம	/	'ma'	as in	mother
மா	/	'm$\bar{a}$'	as in	marsh
மி	/	'mi'	as in	miracle
மீ	/	'm$\bar{\imath}$'	as in	meet
மு	/	'mu'	as in	moustache
மூ	/	'm$\bar{u}$'	as in	moon
மெ	/	'me'	as in	mesh
மே	/	'm$\bar{e}$'	as in	make
மை	/	'mai'	as in	mike
மொ	/	'mo'	as in	monarch
மோ	/	'm$\bar{o}$'	as in	more
மௌ	/	'mau'	as in	mouth

ங் ஞ் ண் ந் ம் ன்

பயிற்சி – EXERCISES

Hierarchy of Skill Acquisition through the following exercises
I. Formation of the letter ♦ II. Correlation of sounds ♦ III. Differentiating between long and short sounds
IV. Reading words as a combination of vowels and consonants of the current series ♦ V. Series Recap

I. Learn to write by tracing the dotted lines completing each character. X = ம

X	Xா	Xி	Xீ		
ம	மா	மி	மீ	மு	மூ
ெX	ேX	ைX	ெXா	ேXா	ெXள
மெ	மே	மை	மொ	மோ	மௌ

II. Listen to the sound of the word and write its closest equivalent Tamil letter.

MY - ☐ ME - ☐

III. Fill in the missing kuril/nedil letters in this incomplete series.

☐	மா	மி	☐	மு	☐
மெ	☐	மை	☐	மோ	மௌ

IV. Read aloud the given words.

அம்மா/AMMĀ/mother	**மை**/MAI/ kajal	**ஆமை**/ĀMAI/tortoise
ஆமாம்/ĀMĀM/yes	**உமி**/UMI/skin of grain	**மாமி**/MĀMI/aunt
இமை/IMAI/ eyebrow	**ஊமை**/ŪMAI/dumb	**மாமா**/MĀMĀ/uncle

V. Fill in the letters of the 'ம்' series.

ம் Series = ம் + (அ, ஆ, இ, ஈ, உ, ஊ, எ, ஏ, ஐ, ஒ, ஓ, ஔ)

= ____,____,____,____,____,____,____,____,____,____,____,____

LESSON - பாடம்

கற்போம் மெல்லினம் / KAṞPŌM MELLIṈAM / Let us learn Mellinam

ன் வரிசை -------------- '(i)ṉ' Series

ன் + அ = ன	(i)ṉ + a = ṉa	ன் + எ = னெ	(i)ṉ + e = ṉe
ன் + ஆ = னா	(i)ṉ + ā = ṉā	ன் + ஏ = னே	(i)ṉ + ē = ṉē
ன் + இ = னி	(i)ṉ + i = ṉi	ன் + ஐ = னை	(i)ṉ + ai = ṉai
ன் + ஈ = னீ	(i)ṉ + ī = ṉī	ன் + ஒ = னொ	(i)ṉ + o = ṉo
ன் + உ = னு	(i)ṉ + u = ṉu	ன் + ஓ = னோ	(i)ṉ + ō = ṉō
ன் + ஊ = னூ	(i)ṉ + ū = ṉū	ன் + ஔ = னௌ	(i)ṉ + au = ṉau

குறில் / kuril / short sound   நெடில் / nedil / long sound

ன்	/	'ṉ'	as in	win
ன	/	'ṉa'	as in	Canada
னா	/	'ṉā'	as in	nonstop
னி	/	'ṉi'	as in	honey
னீ	/	'ṉī'	as in	kneel
னு	/	'ṉu'	as in	Hanuman
னூ	/	'ṉū'	as in	snooty
னெ	/	'ṉe'	as in	channel
னே	/	'ṉē'	as in	nasal
னை	/	'ṉai'	as in	granite
னொ	/	'ṉo'	as in	notation
னோ	/	'ṉō'	as in	anode
னௌ	/	'ṉau'	as in	announce

N.B.

There is no difference in pronunciation between 'ன' (2 circled na) and 'ந' (small na). The difference of usage is meant for orthographic purposes.

பயிற்சி – EXERCISES

Hierarchy of Skill Acquisition through the following exercises
I. Formation of the letter ♦ II. Correlation of sounds ♦ III. Differentiating between long and short sounds
IV. Reading words as a combination of vowels and consonants of the current series ♦ V. Series Recap

I. Learn to write by tracing the dotted lines completing each character. X = ன

X	Xா	Xி	X்		
ன	னா	னி	ன்	னு	னூ
ெX	ேX	ைX	ொX	ோX	ௌX
னெ	னே	னை	னொ	னோ	னௌ

II. Listen to the sound of the word and write its closest equivalent Tamil letter.

ANY - எ____ MINI - மி____

III. Fill in the missing kuril/nedil letters in this incomplete series.

ன		னி		னு	
னெ	னே	னை		னோ	

IV. Read aloud the given words.

அன்னை/**ANNAI/** mother
இனி/**INI**/ hereafter
ஏன்/ĒN/ why
ஊன்/**ŪN/** food
என்ன/**ENNA/** what

V. Fill in the letters of the 'ன்' series.

ன் Series = ன் + (அ, ஆ, இ, ஈ, உ, ஊ, எ, ஏ, ஐ, ஒ, ஓ, ஔ)

= ____,____,____,____,____,____,____,____,____,____,____,____

ங் ஞ் ண் ந் ம் ன்

RECAP : **Mellinam Family: ங/ṅa, ஞ/ña, ண/ṇa, ந/na, ம/ma, ன/n̲a**

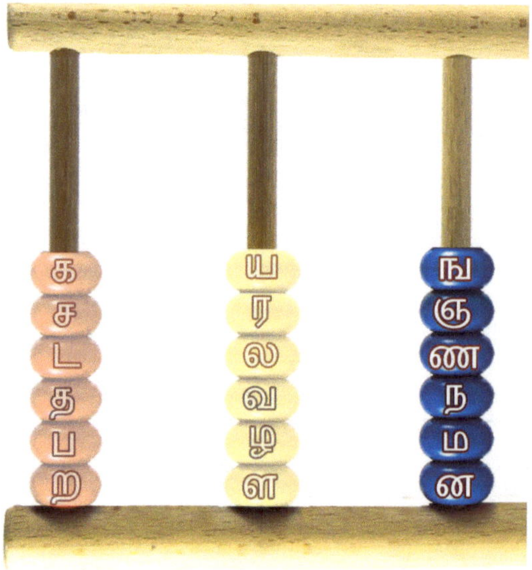

Fill in the missing letters in the table.

	அ	ஆ	இ	ஈ	உ	ஊ	எ	ஏ	ஐ	ஒ	ஓ	ஔ
ங்	ங	ஙா		ஙீ	ஙு		ஙெ	ஙே	ஙை		ஙோ	ஙௌ
ஞ்	ஞ	ஞா	ஞி			ஞூ	ஞெ	ஞே		ஞொ		ஞௌ
ண்	ண		ணி		ணு		ணெ		ணை	ணொ	ணோ	
ந்	ந		நி	நீ	நு	நூ		நே			நோ	நௌ
ம்	ம	மா		மீ	மு		மெ		மை	மொ	மோ	
ன்	ன		னி	னீ		னூ		னே	னை		னோ	னௌ

Now you know how to read the 12 vowels, the Vallinam, the Idaiyinam and the Mellinam family of consonants! From this moment onwards, you should be able to read any Tamil word.

Read out all the words given below:

I Colours : blue/நீலம் yellow/மஞ்சள்

II Numbers : 1/ஒன்று 2/இரண்டு 3/மூன்று
4/நான்கு 5/ஐந்து 9/ஒன்பது

III Body Parts : eye/கண் nose/மூக்கு face/முகம்

ACTIVITY - III

I. Write out the names of these colors in Tamil.

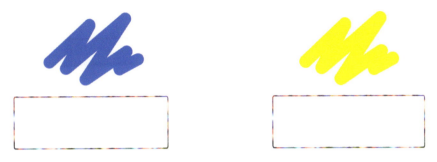

II. Write out the numbers of each of these objects in Tamil.

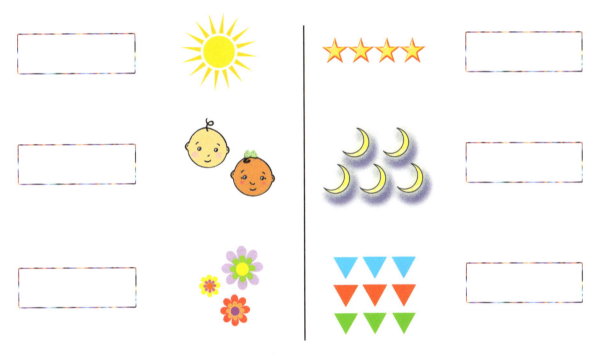

III. Write out the names of parts of the body as indicated in Tamil.

Exercise – Usage of All Tamil Letters

With the help of the pronunciation guide given, write the corresponding Tamil letters to spell the Tamil word for the object shown in the image.

பழங்கள் – Fruits – pazhaṅgaḷ

tomato

tha - (i)k - kā - ḷi

jackfruit

pa - lā - (i)p - pa - zha - (i)m

mango

mā - (i)m - ba - zha - (i)m

gooseberry

ne - (i)l - li - (i)k - kā - (i)y

banana

vā - zhai - (i)p - pa - zha - (i)m

guava

ko - (i)y - yā

custard apple

sī - thā - (i)p - pa - zha - (i)m

chikku fruit

sa - (i)p - pō - (i)ṭ - ṭā

grapes

thi - rā - (i)ṭ - chai

pomegranate

mā - thu - ḷa - (i)m - pa - zha - (i)m

காய்கறிகள் – Vegetables – kāykaṛigal

drumsticks

mu - ru - (i)ṅ - gai - (i)k - kā - (i)y

chilly

mi - ḷa - gā - (i)y

potato

u - ru - ḷai - (i)k - ki - zha - (i)ṅ - ku

raddish

mu - (i)ḷ - ḷa - (i)ṅ - gi

brinjal

ka - (i)th - tha - ri - (i)k - kā - (i)y

onion

ve - (i)ṅ - gā - ya - (i)m

peas

pa - (i)ṭ - ṭā - ṇi

pumpkin

pa - ra - (i)ṅ - gi - (i)k - kā - (i)y

okra

ve - (i)ṇ - ḍai - (i)k - kā - (i)y

spinach

kī - rai

Exercise – Usage of All Tamil Letters

With the help of the pronunciation guide given, write the corresponding Tamil letters to spell the Tamil word for the object shown in the image.

பூக்கள் – Flowers – pūkkaḷ

jasmine

ma - (i)l - li - gai

thā - ma - rai

lotus

marigold

sā - ma - (i)n - dhi

se - (i)m - ba - ru - (i)th - thi

shoeflower

sunflower

sū - ri - ya - gā - (i)n - dhi

thā - zha - (i)m - pū

screwpine flower

– Animals and Birds –

மிருகங்கள் - பறவைகள் mirugaṅgaḷ - paṛavaigaḷ

dog

nā - (i)y

si - (i)ṅ - ga - (i)m

lion

cat

pū - ṉai

pu - ḷi

tiger

monkey

ku - ra - (i)ṅ - gu

ma - yi - (i)l

peacock

mouse

e - li

ka - ra - ḍi

bear

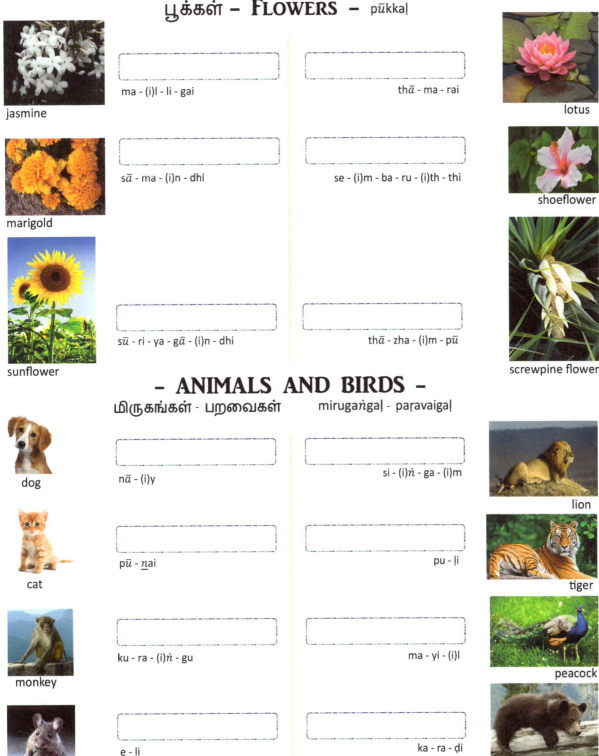

Exercise – Usage of All Tamil Letters

With the help of the pronunciation guide given, write the corresponding Tamil letters to spell the Tamil word for the object shown in the image.

– Animals and Birds (contd) –

மிருகங்கள் - பறவைகள்   mirugaṅgaḷ – paṛavaigaḷ

elephant

yā - ṉai

donkey

ka - zhu - dhai

pigeon

pu - ṛā

crow

kā - (i)k - kai

fish

mī - (i)ṉ

ant

e - ṛu - (i)m - bu

mā - ḍu

cow

ā - ḍu

goat

na - ri

fox

su - ṛā

shark

ā - mai

tortoise

ku - thi - rai

horse

EXERCISE – USAGE OF ALL TAMIL LETTERS

With the help of the pronunciation guide given, write the corresponding Tamil letters to spell the Tamil word for the indicated day/month.

கிழமைகள் – DAYS OF THE WEEK – kizhamaigaḷ

Sunday
gnā - yi - ṛu

Monday
thi - (i)ṅ - ga - (i)ḷ

Tuesday
se - (i)v - vā - (i)y

Wednesday
bu - dha - (i)ṉ

Thursday
vi - ya - zhā - (i)ṉ

Friday
ve - (i)ḷ - ḷi

Saturday
sa - ṉi

தமிழ் மாதங்கள் – TAMIL MONTHS – thamizh mādhaṅgaḷ

mid Apr - mid May
chi - (i)th - thi - rai

mid May - mid Jun
vai - gā - si

mid Jun - mid Jul
ā - ṉi

mid Jul - mid Aug
ā - ḍi

mid Aug - mid Sep
ā - va - ṇi

mid Sep – mid Oct
pu - ra - (i)ṭ - ṭa - si

MID OCT - MID NOV
ai - (i)p - pa - si

mid Nov - mid Dec
kā - (i)r - (i)th - thi - gai

mid Dec - mid Jan
mā - (i)r - ga - zhi

MID JAN - MID FEB
thai

MID FEB - MID MAR
mā - si

mid MAR - mid APR
pa - (i)ṅ - gu - ṉi

நன்றி - Thank You   வணக்கம் - Greetings   தமிழகம் - Tamil Nadu

Ayudha Letter

ஆயுத எழுத்து - ஃ *Āyudha* **Ezhuthu - ("ahk")**

எந்த உச்சரிப்புக்கு பயன்படுத்தலாம்?

What is its use with respect to pronunciation?

If it is written before "ga"/'க' or "dha"/'த', it gives the sound "h"/'ஹ்'.

Examples:

எஃகு/ehgu/ iron   இஃது/ihdhu/this

அஃது/ahdhu/that   அஃறிணை/ ahkriṇai/ all living and non-living things except humans

If it is written before "ja"/ 'ஜ', then 'ஜ'/ "ja" sound is converted into "za".

Example: அஃஜாருதீன்/Azharudheen   ஃஜாம்பியா/Zambia

If is written before "pa" /ப, then 'ப'/"pa" sound is converted into "pha/fa".

Examples:

ஃப்ரான்ஸ்/france	காஃபி/coffee	ஃபோன்/phone
ஃபலூடா/faloda	ஆஃப்கன்/Afkhan	ஃபிலிப்/philip
ஃபாஸில்/fossil	ஃபைல்/file	ஃப்ளோரிடா/Florida
ஃபேக்ஸ்/fax,	ஃபைன்/fine	ஃபாஸ்ட்/fast
ஃபீனிக்ஸ்/phoenix	ஃபன்/fun	ஃபைல்/file
ஃபானிக்ஸ்/phonics	ஃபேன்/fan	ஃப்ரெஷ்/fresh

Basically it is used to represent the sound "za" and "pha/fa" from English phonetics.

சிறப்பு எழுத்துக்கள் / Siṛappu Ezhuthukkaḷ / Special Letters

ஸ்ரீ, க்ஷ, ஜ, ஸ, ஹ, ஷ

	க்ஷ (க்+ஷ) ksh (k + sh)	ஜ் (j)	ஸ் (s)	ஹ் (h)	ஷ் (sh)
அ	க்ஷ/ksha	ஜ/ja	ஸ/sa	ஹ/ha	ஷ/sha
ஆ	க்ஷா/kshā	ஜா/jā	ஸா/sā	ஹா/hā	ஷா/shā
இ	க்ஷி/kshi	ஜி/ji	ஸி/si	ஹி/hi	ஷி/shi
ஈ	க்ஷீ/kshī	ஜீ/jī	ஸீ/sī	ஹீ/hī	ஷீ/shī
உ	க்ஷு/kshu	ஜு/ju	ஸு/su	ஹு/hu	ஷு/shu
ஊ	க்ஷூ/kshū	ஜூ/jū	ஸூ/sū	ஹூ/hū	ஷூ/shū
எ	க்ஷெ/kshe	ஜெ/je	ஸெ/se	ஹெ/he	ஷெ/she
ஏ	க்ஷே/kshē	ஜே/jē	ஸே/sē	ஹே/hē	ஷே/shē
ஐ	க்ஷை/kshai	ஜை/jai	ஸை/sai	ஹை/hai	ஷை/shai
ஒ	க்ஷொ/ksho	ஜொ/jo	ஸொ/so	ஹொ/ho	ஷொ/sho
ஓ	க்ஷோ/kshō	ஜோ/jō	ஸோ/sō	ஹோ/hō	ஷோ/shō
ஔ	க்ஷௌ/kshau	ஜௌ/jau	ஸௌ/sau	ஹௌ/hau	ஷௌ/shau

Examples for க்ஷ்/Ksha: Rikshaw, Kshemam, Subhiksham, Laksham, Sakshi

Examples for ஜ்/Ja: Jade, Joy, Jolly, Joke, Jeans, Juice, July, Jasmine, Jeep

Examples for ஸ்/Sa: Snake, Master, Miss, Hissing, Silly, Visa, Resort

Examples for ஹ்/Ha: Hall, He, Heel, Who, Hen, Hyderabad, How, Hire, Himachal

Examples for ஷ்/Sha: Ship, She, Shoe, Shake, Shine, Sharp, Shore, Shield, Show

ஸ்ரீ / Sri - Indicates respectful title

Example: Sri Ram, Sri Mukham

Answer Key

வல்லினம் II Correlation of the sound

Pg 7:	Cow/கௌ	Go/கோ	Guy/கை	Key/கீ
Pg 9:	Sea/சீ	Saw/சா	So/சோ	
Pg 11:	Tie/டை	Tea/டீ	Day/டே	
Pg 13:	Thigh/தை	They/தே	The/த	
Pg 15:	Pie/பை	Bye/பை	Bee/பீ	
Pg 17:	Christmas/க்றிஸ்துமஸ்	Curry/கறி		

இடையினம் II Correlation of the sound

Pg 21:	You/யூ	Yo-yo/யோ-யோ	
Pg 23:	Ray/ரே	Raw/ரா	Row/ரோ
Pg 25:	Law/லா	Low/லோ	Lay/லே
Pg 27:	Way/வே	We/வீ	Why/வை
Pg 29:	Yaazh/யாழ்	Thamizh/தமிழ்	
Pg 30:	Glue/க்ளு	Blow/ப்ளோ	

மெல்லினம் II Correlation of the sound

Pg 35:	Song/சாங்	Wrong/ராங்
Pg 37:	Angel/ஏஞ்சல்	Range/ரேஞ்ச்
Pg 39:	Money/மணி	
Pg 41:	No/நோ	Now/நௌ
Pg 43:	My/மை	Me/மீ
Pg 45:	Any/எனி	Mini/மினி

Pg 48:

Fruits

1. தக்காளி 2. மாம்பழம் 3. வாழைப்பழம் 4. சீதாப்பழம் 5. திராட்சை
6. பலாப்பழம் 7. நெல்லிக்காய் 8. கொய்யா 9. சப்போட்டா 10. மாதுளம்பழம்

Vegetables

1. முருங்கைக்காய் 2. உருளைக்கிழங்கு 3. கத்தரிக்காய் 4. பட்டாணி 5. வெண்டைக்காய்
6. மிளகாய் 7. முள்ளங்கி 8. வெங்காயம் 9. பரங்கிக்காய் 10. கீரை

Pg 49:

Flowers

1. மல்லிகை 2. சாமந்தி 3. சூரியகாந்தி 4. தாமரை 5. செம்பருத்தி 6. தாழம்பூ

Animals and Birds

1. நாய் 2. பூனை 3. கரடி 4. எலி 5. சிங்கம் 6. புலி 7. மயில் 8. குரங்கு

Pg 50:

Animals and Birds (contd)

1. யானை 2. கழுதை 3. புறா 4. காக்கை 5. மீன் 6. எறும்பு
7. மாடு 8. ஆடு 9. நரி 10. சுறா 11. ஆமை 12. குதிரை

Pg 51:

Days of the Week

1. ஞாயிறு 2. திங்கள் 3. செவ்வாய் 4. புதன் 5. வியாழன் 6. வெள்ளி 7. சனி

Tamil Months

1. சித்திரை 2. வைகாசி 3. ஆனி 4. ஆடி 5. ஆவணி 6. புரட்டாசி
7. ஐப்பசி 8. கார்த்திகை 9. மார்கழி 10. தை 11. மாசி 12. பங்குனி

CONGRATULATIONS!!!

You have mastered the Tamil letters!

TABLE OF TAMIL LETTERS IN ALPHABETICAL ORDER

	ahk	a	ā	i	ī	u	ū	e	ē	ai	o	ō	au
	ஃ	அ	ஆ	இ	ஈ	உ	ஊ	எ	ஏ	ஐ	ஒ	ஓ	ஔ
(i)k	க்	க	கா	கி	கீ	கு	கூ	கெ	கே	கை	கொ	கோ	கௌ
(i)ṅ	ங்	ங	ஙா	ஙி	ஙீ	ஙு	ஙூ	ஙெ	ஙே	ஙை	ஙொ	ஙோ	ஙௌ
(i)ch	ச்	ச	சா	சி	சீ	சு	சூ	செ	சே	சை	சொ	சோ	சௌ
(i)ñ	ஞ்	ஞ	ஞா	ஞி	ஞீ	ஞு	ஞூ	ஞெ	ஞே	ஞை	ஞொ	ஞோ	ஞௌ
(i)ṭ	ட்	ட	டா	டி	டீ	டு	டூ	டெ	டே	டை	டொ	டோ	டௌ
(i)ṇ	ண்	ண	ணா	ணி	ணீ	ணு	ணூ	ணெ	ணே	ணை	ணொ	ணோ	ணௌ
(i)th	த்	த	தா	தி	தீ	து	தூ	தெ	தே	தை	தொ	தோ	தௌ
(i)n	ந்	ந	நா	நி	நீ	நு	நூ	நெ	நே	நை	நொ	நோ	நௌ
(i)p	ப்	ப	பா	பி	பீ	பு	பூ	பெ	பே	பை	பொ	போ	பௌ
(i)m	ம்	ம	மா	மி	மீ	மு	மூ	மெ	மே	மை	மொ	மோ	மௌ
(i)y	ய்	ய	யா	யி	யீ	யு	யூ	யெ	யே	யை	யொ	யோ	யௌ
(i)r	ர்	ர	ரா	ரி	ரீ	ரு	ரூ	ரெ	ரே	ரை	ரொ	ரோ	ரௌ
(i)l	ல்	ல	லா	லி	லீ	லு	லூ	லெ	லே	லை	லொ	லோ	லௌ
(i)v	வ்	வ	வா	வி	வீ	வு	வூ	வெ	வே	வை	வொ	வோ	வௌ
(i)zh	ழ்	ழ	ழா	ழி	ழீ	ழு	ழூ	ழெ	ழே	ழை	ழொ	ழோ	ழௌ
(i)ḷ	ள்	ள	ளா	ளி	ளீ	ளு	ளூ	ளெ	ளே	ளை	ளொ	ளோ	ளௌ
(i)ṟ	ற்	ற	றா	றி	றீ	று	றூ	றெ	றே	றை	றொ	றோ	றௌ
(i)ṉ	ன்	ன	னா	னி	னீ	னு	னூ	னெ	னே	னை	னொ	னோ	னௌ

(Vowel) Uyir Ezhuthu + (Consonant) Mei Ezhuthu = Uyir Mei Ezhuthu

Uyir Ezhuthukkal	:	12
Mei Ezhuthukkal	:	18
Uyir Mei Ezhuthukkal	:	12 x 18 = 216
Ayudha Ezhuthu	:	1
Total no. of Letters	:	12 + 18 + 216 + 1 = 247

SAY IT TO WIN IT!

சொல்க - வெல்க

No. of Players: 2 - 4

Objective: To win the crown with the highest points

Game Preparation:

1. Make a single die with 4 values : 1, 2, 3 and a monkey face.

(OR)

Use pistachio shells or a wooden block and write the value on each shell with a marker. You can also use cards (ace for 1, 2, 3 and joker for the monkey) and so on.

2. Use a small item to represent the player (an eraser, paperclip, colored paper, etc).
3. A paper and pen/pencil to keep score
4. Tamil-English dictionary (optional)

Rules:

1. **From START to Vowel tree:**
   - All players place their pieces at START. Roll the die on your turn.
   - Players that get the monkey, **move to the vowel apple tree**.
   - Other players stay at START until they roll a monkey on their turn.
2. **From Vowel Tree to Training Hut:**
   - Roll the die.
   - Pick the number of vowels as per what you roll and move to the training hut.

- Pick the same number of consonants.
- Combine the vowels and consonants to get the corresponding Tamil letters.
- Say aloud a word starting with each of the Tamil letters.
- For every correct word, you earn 100 points.
- *If you roll a monkey on your turn, you must pick 5 vowels from the vowel tree and 5 consonants from the training hut. Combine to form 5 letters. Say aloud 5 words starting with the letters. If all of them are said correctly, you earn 500 points.

3. From Training Hut to Pond Entry

- You will earn 100 points for every correct word and move that many grey tiles at the entry of the pond.
- *Move directly to the first tile of the ruby set if:

  You have rolled a monkey on your previous turn and said aloud 5 words correctly.

  Refer previous point if you do not say all 5 words correctly.

4. From Grey Tiles to Topaz Tiles

- Roll the die.
- Say a Tamil word from the book and move across each tile according to the number and depending on how many words are said correctly.

  For example: If you roll a 3, say three words and move across three tiles. If you get only two words right, you can move only two tiles.

  a) If you land directly on a connecting pebble with the alligator sign next to it, you will be caught by the alligator. You have to move to the training hut.

(Note: The first connecting pebble before the ruby series requires no challenge.)

On your next turn, complete the exercise given at the training hut successfully and roll the die. Move from where you left off.

(Note: Training hut exercises are explained below the alligator challenges.)

If you do not complete the exercise correctly, you will need to stay at the training hut and try again on your next turn.

b) If you get to cross the connecting pebble to complete your move, you have to take up an alligator challenge (which will be decided by your opponent).

If you successfully complete the challenge, you can move past it. If you make a mistake, you have two options:-

i. Go to the training hut. Complete an exercise on your next turn. Roll the die and move from where you left off. **(OR)**

ii. Pass the connecting pebble but miss your next two turns.

c) If you land on a gem tile (ruby, emerald, sapphire, topaz tiles), your opponent dictates two Tamil words for you to write.

Each correctly written word = 100 points

d) If you land on a grey tile with a gem stone engraved in it, you can choose any one word from the book and write it to earn 100 points. If the word is not written correctly, you don't earn any points.

e) **If you land on a tile that is occupied by another player**, the other player is pushed back to the starting tile of the gem series they were currently on.

- If you roll a monkey, you get a bonus of 500 points and move to the starting tile of the next gem series and repeat (d).

  You must also take the alligator challenge and follow the same procedure as (b).

5. **From Topaz Tiles to Golden Tiles**

- While on the topaz series, if you roll a number that gets you past the final grey tile, you will have to stop at the bridge.
- You can cross the bridge and reach the first golden tile ONLY when you roll a monkey.
- Until you get the monkey pass, you stay on the topaz series.

6. **From Golden Tiles to Lotus**

- Roll the die and recite lines from the Aathichudi. The number of lines you recite depends on the number rolled.
- If you roll a monkey, and your opponent is further ahead of you:

  You can swap positions to take the lead.
- If you roll a monkey and you are already at the lead:

  You can move to the WIN tile.
- On the win tile, you must recite 6 lines of the Aathichudi to reach the crown.
- **If you make mistakes on any of the turns,** return to the first golden tile.
- You must roll the exact number to reach the win tile. Until then, you stay in your current position.
- **The first to reach the crown wins 1000 points.**

  The second one to reach earns **500 points**. The third earns **200 points**.
- If the last player is on the golden tile while the previous player reaches the crown, he earns 100 points. If he is still on the grey tiles, he is out of the game.

The player at the crown with the most points wins!

ALLIGATOR CHALLENGES

1. Select a vowel and say all the consonants in combination of the vowel in alphabetical order. (Ex: chosen vowel இ: கி ஙி சி ஞி டி ணி தி நி பி மி யி ரி லி வி ழி ளி றி னி)
2. Say two words and obtain the vowel sounds from the words. (Ex: மகிழ்ச்சி - அ from ம, இ from கி, இ from சி)
3. Say a pair of rhyming words.
4. Say any two words indicating an action.
5. Say a pair of words in which one uses a kuril sound and the other using the same letter with the nedil sound. (Ex: அண்ணி, ஆணி: அ/ஆ ; முந்திரி, மூக்கு: மு/மூ)
6. Say a pair of words, one using the letters of the "ல்" series and the other using the letters of the "ள்" series. Be careful to distinguish the sounds correctly!
7. Say a pair of opposites.
8. Say a pair of words, one using the letter of the "ற்" series and the other having a "ற்ற" combination. Be careful to distinguish the sounds correctly! (Ex: சிறகு, சற்று)
9. Say a pair of words, one using the letters of the "ழ்" series and the other using the "ஞ்" series.
10. Say a word containing another word hidden in it. (Ex: வாழ்க்கை – வாழ் or கை)

Training Hut Exercises

Refer the book if you need help completing any of the exercises.

a) Write the series of any consonant that your opponent chooses. **(OR)**

b) Write 3 words which your opponent will dictate. **(OR)**

c) Pick any five vowels and you must say a word starting with that vowel sound combined with any consonant. (Ex: அ : கணக்கு) – Refer Rangu's guide

RANGU'S GUIDE!

CHALLENGE 1

Alphabetical Order : க் ங் ச் ஞ் ட் ண் த் ந் ப் ம் ய் ர் ல் வ் ழ் ள் ற் ன்

CHALLENGE 2

Mother–அம்மா–அ ஆ
Father–அப்பா–அ ஆ
Younger brother–தம்பி–அ இ
Younger sister–தங்கை–அ ஐ
Letter–எழுத்து–எ உ உ
Sun–சூரியன்–ஊ இ அ
Moon–நிலா–இ ஆ
Tamil–தமிழ்–அ இ
Word–சொல்–ஒ
Wet–ஈரம்–ஈ அ
Help–உதவி–உ அ இ

Home–வீடு–ஈ உ
Wealth–செல்வம்–எ அ
Speed–வேகம்–ஏ அ
Crush–நொறுக்கு–ஒ உ உ
Pick out–பொறுக்கு–ஒ உ உ
Pattern–கோலம்–ஓ அ
Full moon–பௌர்ணமி–ஔ அ இ
Veenai–வீணை–ஈ ஐ
Valour–வீரம்–ஈ அ
Human–மனிதன்–அ இ அ
Monkey–குரங்கு–உ அ

CHALLENGE 3

யானை–பானை (elephant–pot)
கனி–பனி (fruit–snow)
சிறை–பிறை (prison–crescent moon)
புருவம்–உருவம் (eyebrow–form)
படிப்பு–நடிப்பு (studies–acting)
உடை–குடை (apparel–umbrella)
தேங்காய்–மாங்காய் (coconut–raw mango)
பேச்சு–மூச்சு (speech–breath)
தங்கம்–சிங்கம் (gold–lion)
அலை–வலை (wave–net)
இழு–புழு (pull–worm)
நெற்றி–வெற்றி (forehead–victory)
தரை–கரை (floor–color)
பயிர்–தயிர் (crop–curd)
கண்ணீர்–தண்ணீர் (tears–water)
பாடல்–ஆடல் (song–dance)
நரி–கரி (fox–coal)
ஓது–மோது (chant–go up against)

கடை–படை (shop–army)
பை–மை (bag–eyeliner)
வேகம்–மேகம் (speed–cloud)
கண்–மண் (eye–soil)
காடு–நாடு (forest–nation)
எண்ணை–வெண்ணை (oil–butter)
வினா–கனா (question–dream)
வெயில்–மயில் (sunny–peacock)
குரல்–விரல் (voice–finger)
மலை–தலை (mountain–head)
தள்ளு–அள்ளு (push–gather)
ஆடு–மாடு (goat–cow)
காட்சி–ஆட்சி (vision–governance)
விறகு–சிறகு (firewood–feather)
ஆசை–ஓசை (desire–sound)
அழி–குழி (erase–pit)
பல்–கல் (tooth–stone)
கோடு–தோடு (line–earring)

CHALLENGE 4

படி–read	பாடு–sing	ஆடு–dance	கொடு–give	வாங்கு–get
விற்பனை–sale	தா–give	தூங்கு–sleep	கவனி–observe	பொறு–wait
காத்திடு–protect	ஓடு–run	நடி–act	பேசு–talk	குதி–jump
ஏறு–climb up	யோசி–think	உழை–work	கேள்–hear/ask	பார்–see
துவை–wash	சிரி–laugh	ஓட்டு–drive	செய்–do	எழுந்திரு–wake up
இறங்கு–climb down	போ–go	வா–come	விற்றுவிடு–sell	விளையாடு–play

CHALLENGE 5

அசை–move	ஆசை–desire
படம்–picture	பாடம்–lesson
சிலை–idol	சீலை–curtain
விடு–leave	வீடு–house
நிலம்–land	நீலம்–blue
கொடு–give	கோடு–line
தொடு–touch	தோடு–ear stud
பசி–hunger	பாசி–moss
பல–many	பலா–jack fruit
பதி–husband	பாதி–half
மிதி–stomp	மீதி–balance,
மடு–valley	மாடு–bull
விதி–fate/rule,	வீதி–street,
குடை–umbrella	கூடை–basket
குரல்–voice	கூறல்–telling
வரம்–boon	வாரம்–week
அணி–team	ஆணி–nail (tool)
குறை–complaint	கூறை–roof
அரிசி–rice	ஆசி–blessing
மலை–mountain	மாலை–garland/evening

CHALLENGE 6

அவள்–she	அவல்–puffed rice	வால்–tail	வாள்–sword,	தலை–head
தளை–hand cuffs	விலை–price	விளை–yield	கலை-art	களை–weed
நீலம்–blue	நீளம்–length	போலி–fake	கலம்–bowl	களம்–field
மூலை–corner	மூளை–brain	வெல்லம்–jaggery	வெள்ளம்–flood	புலி–tiger
புளி–tamarind	புள்ளி–dot	எள்–sesame	பல்–tooth	வெள்ளை–white
இளமை–youth	வெள்ளி–silver	வலி–pain	பல்கலைக்கழகம்–university	கொள்ளை–robbery
பல்லி–lizard	துளி–drop	முள்–thorn	நீங்கல்–eliminate	நீங்கள்–you (with respect)
பள்ளி–school	வெள்ளாடு–white goat	குள்ளன்–dwarf		

CHALLENGE 7

மேலே x கீழே (above x below)	வினா x விடை (question x answer)
சிரி x அழு (laugh x cry)	குளிர் x வெப்பம் (chillness x heat)
நில் x உட்கார் (stand x sit)	நண்பன் x பகைவன் (friend x enemy)
திற x மூடு (open x close)	வெற்றி x தோல்வி (success x failure)
கனிவு x கடுமை (kind x rude)	அன்பு x வெறுப்பு (love x hatred)
தூக்கம் x விழிப்பு (sleep x awake)	இனிப்பு x கசப்பு (sweet x bitter)
உள்ளே x வெளியே (inside x outside)	மெதுவாக x வேகமாக (slow x fast)
ஏறு x இறங்கு (climb up x climb down)	கொடுத்தல் x வாங்குதல் (giving x buying)
வரலாம் x போகலாம் (can come x can go)	வரவு x செலவு (credit x debit)
உயரம் x குள்ளம் (tall x short)	இன்பம் x துன்பம் (pleasure x misery)
மெய் x பொய் (truth x lie)	போதும் x வேண்டும் (sufficient x insufficient)
சிறிய x பெரிய (small x big)	ஆரம்பம் x முடிவு (beginning x ending)
குறைவு x அதிகம் (less x more)	பழையது X புதியது (old x new)

CHALLENGE 8

காற்று–wind	நேற்று–yesterday	பற்று–attached	மற்றவை–others
சிற்றுந்து–small bus	விற்றல்–selling	கற்றல்–learning	சுற்றுதல்–circling
கற்காலம்–stone age	பொற்காலம்–golden age	பொற்றாமரை–golden lotus	பற்பசை–toothpaste
சொற்கள்–words	விற்பனை–sale	பெற்றோர்–parent	புற்று–ant hill
மாற்றம்–change	சிற்பம்–sculpture	கற்றாழை–aloe vera	பொற்பேழை–golden box
அற்புதம்–miracle	சீற்றம்–fury	மற்போர்–wrestling	கற்பனை–imagination
கற்சிலை–stone idol	நாற்றம்–smell	தெற்கு–south	மேற்கு–west
நூற்றாண்டு–centenary year	கற்கண்டு–rock sugar		

CHALLENGE 9

இஞ்சி–ginger	பஞ்சு–cotton	பஞ்சம்–scarcity	மஞ்சள்–yellow/turmeric
அஞ்சறைப்பெட்டி–spice box	அஞ்சனம்–eye liner	ஞாயிறு–Sunday	ஞாபகம்–memory
ஞானம்–wisdom	கொஞ்சம்–few	எஞ்சியது–left over	நெஞ்சம்–heart
கொஞ்சு–petting	கஞ்சம்–miser	கெஞ்சு–beg	அஞ்சாமை–fearless
விஞ்சுதல்–surpass	அஞ்சல்–post	செஞ்சிலுவை–red cross	

(OR)

குழந்தை–child	வாழை–banana	பழம்–fruit	விழி–eye	மொழி–language
பழி–revenge	கொழுப்பு–fat	இழப்பு–loss	அழுத்தம்–pressure	அழுக்கு–dirt
பழகுதல்–mingle	தாழ்–lock	சோழி–cowrie shell	அழகு–beauty	கழுத்து–neck
வழிதல்–overflowing	விழுதல்–falling	அழுகை–cry	செழிப்பு–wealth	அழைப்பு–invitation
இதழ்கள்–petals	கிழமை–day	இழு–pull	எழு–wake up	பழக்கம்–habit
வழுக்கு–slippery				

CHALLENGE 10

வானரம்–வாரம் (monkey–week)	கானகம்–காகம் (forest–crow)	நாடகம்–நாகம் (drama–snake)
மாதுளை–துளை (pomegranate–hole)	சிலந்தி–சிந்தி (spider–think)	மரகதம்–மரம் (emerald–tree)
விளையாடு–விடு (play–leave)	சிகரம்–சிரம், கரம் (peak–head, hand)	உணர்வு–உணவு (feeling–food)
மகுடம்–குடம் (crown–pot)	கரும்பு–கம்பு (sugarcane–kambu millet)	அரும்பு–அம்பு (bud–arrow)
மக்கள்–மகள் (people–daughter)	பாடல்–பால் (song–milk)	வாகனம்–வானம்/கனம் (vehicle–sky, weight)
அப்படி–படி (like that–stair/read)	விடுதலை–விலை(freedom from something–price)	நகரம்–நகம்(city–fingernail)
ஆரம்பம்–ரம்பம் (beginning–saw tool)	பாடல்–பால் (song – milk)	வளையல்–வயல்(bangle–fields)
வேர்க்கடலை–வேர்/கலை/வேலை(peanut–root/art/work)		

GUIDE TO TRAINING HUT ACTIVITY (C)

அ	பருப்பு - dhal, பழம் - fruit, வண்ணம் - color, கருப்பு – black, கலை - art, சரித்திரம் - history, நடிப்பு - acting, படிப்பு - studies, தனிமை - solitude, அரிசி - rice
ஆ	ஆசை - desire, பாடு - sing, ஆடல் - dance, காரம் - spicy, சாலை - road, தாகம் - thirst, வாரம் - week, ராணி - queen, நாடு - country, ஆயிரம் - thousand
இ	இசை - music, கிளி - parrot, சிங்கம் - lion, திருடன் - thief, விலை - price, மின்னல் - lightning, பிறப்பு - birth, நிமிடம் – minute, மின்சாரம் - electricity, கிளை - branch
ஈ	கீரை - spinach, சீப்பு - comb, தீர்வு - solution, வீதி - street, நீளம் - long, நீர் - water, மீதம் - leftover, சீறுதல் - hissing, மீண்டும் – again, நீதி - justice
உ	உலகம் - world, குடை - umbrella, துணி - cloth, புன்னகை - smile, முகம் – face துணை – companion, முடிவு - ending, நுரை - froth, சுமை - load, குளம் - pond
ஊ	சூடு - hot, தூய்மை - cleanliness, தூரம் - far, பூக்கள் - flowers, பூனை - cat மூளை - brain, நூறு - hundred, மூடி - lid, நூலகம் - library, நூல் - thread
எ	எண் - number, செல்வம் - riches, வெங்காயம் - onion, வெப்பம் - heat, பெண் - woman, மெத்தை - mattress, நெல் - paddy, பெயர் – name, நெருப்பு – fire, எலும்பு - bone
ஏ	ஏணி - ladder, கேள்வி - question, சேமி - save, தேன் - honey, தேங்காய் - coconut, வேகம் - speed, வேர் - root, நேரம் - time, மேகம் - cloud, மேடை - stage
ஐ	ஐம்பது - fifty, தையல் - stitch, கைத்தடி – walking stick, மைனா – mynah bird, பைசா - coin, பைத்தியம் - mental, வைத்தியம் – treatment (for an illness), ஐம்பூதங்கள் – 5 elements, பையன் - boy, கைதி - prisoner
ஒ	சொந்தம் - owned, கொம்பு - horn, தொடர் - series, பொறுமை - patience, பொடி - powder, பொறாமை – jealousy, மொட்டு - bud, கொண்டாட்டம் - celebration, பொன் - gold, கொக்கு - stork
ஓ	ஓசை - sound, கோடு - line, சோதனை - experiment, போர்க்களம் – war field, யோசனை - idea, மோது - crash, நோய் - disease, மோர் - buttermilk, மோப்பம் – sniff out, போதும் - enough
ஔ	மௌனம் - silence, பௌர்ணமி – full moon, யௌவனம் - youthful, ஔடதம் - medicine, சௌக்கியம் - wellbeing, வௌவால் – bat (animal), ரௌத்திரம் – anger, கௌரவம் - prestige

ஔவை ஆத்திச்சூடி	Auvai Aathichudi
அறம் செய விரும்பு	Desire to do good deeds.
ஆறுவது சினம்	Anger should be controlled.
இயல்வது கரவேல்	Be helpful to the best possible extent.
ஈவது விலக்கேல்	Don't stop doing charity.
உடையது விளம்பேல்	Do not boast about your possessions.
ஊக்கமது கைவிடேல்	Do not give up hope/self confidence.
எண் எழுத்து இகழேல்	Do not underestimate the power of learning.
ஏற்பது இகழ்ச்சி	To accept alms is a shameful act.
ஐயம் இட்டு உண்	Before you eat, share food with those in need.
ஒப்புரவு ஒழுகு	Act with high moral standards.
ஓதுவது ஒழியேல்	Never stop learning.
ஔவியம் பேசேல்	Do not talk bad about others.
அஃகஞ் சுருக்கேல்	Do not be stingy in selling food grains.

பாரதியார் ஆத்திச்சூடி	Bharathiyar Aathichudi
அச்சம் தவிர்	Be fearless.
ஆண்மை தவறேல்	Never lack boldness.
இளைத்தல் இகழ்ச்சி	Weakness is pitiful.
ஈகை திறன்	Practice benevolence.
உடலினை உறுதி செய்	Take care of your physical health.
ஊண்மிக விரும்பு	Relish food.
எண்ணுவ துயர்வு	Think positive.
ஏறுபோல் நட	Walk with your head held high.
ஐம்பொறி ஆட்சி கொள்	Govern your senses.
ஒற்றுமை வலிமையாம்	Unity is strength.
ஓய்த லொழி	Don't be lazy.
ஔடதங் குறை	Cut down on medicine.

இன்னுமொரு ஆத்திச்சூடி	One more Aathichudi
அடக்கம் பழகு	Practice humility.
ஆர்வமொடு படி	Learn with enthusiasm.
இனிமையாய்ப் பேசு	Speak with kindness.
ஈவிரக்கம் கொள்	Be compassionate.
உள்ளம் நிறைவு பெறு	Have a content heart.
ஊர் உயர நன்மைசெய்	Contribute good things to your city.
எளிமை விரும்பு	Prefer simplicity.
ஏற்றம் அடைய உழை	Work hard to achieve heights.
ஐயம் தெளியத் தேடு	Search and seek answers to all your doubts.
ஒன்றிணைந்து வாழ்	Live in harmony.
ஓதுவார்தமை மதி	Respect the learned ones.
ஔடதம் உணவென்று அறி	Know that true medicine is food.
இஃதே வாழ்வின் நெறி	These are the virtues of life.

CUT AND PASTE ON CHART TO
MAKE YOUR OWN GAME BOARD

க்
ச்
ட்
ய்
ர்
ல்
வ்
ழ்
ள்
த்
ப்
ற்
to pond
training
← hut
ங்
ஞ்
ந்
ன்
ம்
ண்
இ
ஆ
ஈ
ஊ
அ
உ
ஓ
எ
ஏ
ஒ
ஐ
ஔ
Hi! I'M Rangu, Wanna play?
welcome
vowel tree
pond
START

to hut
Need Some Help?
!
WIN

Printed in the USA
CPSIA information can be obtained
at www.ICGtesting.com
LVHW060710110923
757787LV00091B/69